FROM THE LIBRARY OF
Pat Barry

CHRISTOPHER WARWICK

ABDICATION

SIDGWICK & JACKSON
LONDON

First published in Great Britain in 1986
by Sidgwick & Jackson Limited

Copyright © 1986 by Christopher Warwick

Picture research by Anne-Marie Ehrlich

ISBN 0–283–99351–0

Phototypeset by Falcon Graphic Art Ltd
Wallington, Surrey
Printed in Great Britain by Butler & Tanner Limited,
Frome, Somerset
for Sidgwick & Jackson Limited
1 Tavistock Chambers, Bloomsbury Way
London WC1A 2SG

CONTENTS

ACKNOWLEDGEMENTS

Of all those who have given me assistance in ways too numerous and diverse to specify, in the course of writing this book, I am particularly indebted to Mr Hugo Vickers, whose kindness and extreme generosity I profoundly appreciate. I am no less grateful to the Lady Elizabeth Anson, the Lady Alexandra Metcalfe, the Honourable Mrs Angela Lascelles, and Mr Kenneth Rose, to whom I extend my very deepest thanks.

I would also like to acknowledge, with much gratitude, each of the following: Mr Brian Auld, Mrs Doreen Montgomery, the Honourable Gerald Lascelles, Dr Robert Baldock, Ms Anne-Marie Ehrlich, Mr Michael Shea, Mr John Haslam, Mrs Netty Forshaw, Mr Ralph Selby, Mrs Muriel Scadding, Mr Frank S. FitzGerald-Bush, Mrs Hilary Close, and Mrs Jane Marsh. Towards the end of my research, the present owners of Fort Belvedere, who have asked not to be named, permitted me to walk round the house and garden so greatly loved by HRH The Duke of Windsor, both as Prince of Wales and as King. That my visit occurred, albeit coincidentally, at the time of the forty-ninth anniversary of the Abdication made it all the more poignant.

At Sidgwick & Jackson, my warmest thanks must go to Mr Nigel Newton, whose idea this book was, Mr William Armstrong, for inviting – and then persuading – me to write it, my editor Ms Carey Smith, Ms Katrina Ure, and Ms Kerry Hood.

To those who have asked to remain anonymous, or indeed, to anyone I may inadvertently have overlooked, may I simply say a heartfelt thank-you.

Christopher Warwick

May 1986

For
R W B

*

PROLOGUE

With the death of King George V on 20 January 1936, his eldest son, Edward, Prince of Wales, ascended the throne as His Majesty King Edward VIII. Eleven months later, on Thursday 10 December, the new sovereign subscribed his signature to a document dramatically headed 'Instrument of Abdication'. The following afternoon, while lunching with Winston Churchill at Fort Belvedere – his private retreat at Sunningdale, on the very edge of Windsor Great Park – Edward ceased to reign.

Shortly after 2 a.m. on Saturday 12 December, the King who had preferred to renounce his throne rather than sacrifice his love for Mrs Wallis Simpson, an American divorcee, left England aboard the battleship HMS *Fury*, to cross the Channel to France. From there he journeyed on to Vienna, arriving on Monday the fourteenth. Waiting at the railway station to greet his former sovereign was Sir Walford Selby, Britain's Ambassador to Austria.

As if searching for an identity, or at least for reassurance that he still had one, the first question the ex-King asked was, 'What is my name?'

Sir Walford replied, 'Sir, you are His Royal Highness The Duke of Windsor.'

– 1 –

PRINCE EDWARD

AS PRINCE OF WALES, he held an entire empire spellbound; as King, he scandalized the world by his abdication; and as Duke of Windsor, he chose to spend the last thirty-five years of his life wandering aimlessly in a hinterland of exile. His story begins at White Lodge, Richmond Park, Surrey, on Midsummer's Eve, 23 June 1894.

The first child of the future King George V and Queen Mary, then Duke and Duchess of York, the infant prince was named Edward Albert Christian George Andrew Patrick David, the last four in diplomatic tribute to the patron saints of Great Britain. He was born into a family whose members revolved, like a myriad small satellites, round a seemingly eternal, but slowly setting, sun. Britannia still ruled the waves unrivalled; vast areas of the world's surface were painted imperial red, and from Windsor, Victoria, Queen and Empress, great-grandmother of the newest Prince of York, reigned supreme.

At the age of seventy-five, the Queen had just entered the fifty-eighth year of a reign that would ultimately span sixty-four years and would witness the dawn of a century of transformation. Most of the thrones occupied by her crowned descendants would be swept away – by war, revolution, or the spread of republicanism – and indeed the survival of the very throne she had occupied since 1837 would be threatened by the great-grandson whose nativity had given her such profound pleasure.

Shortly after Prince Edward's birth, Queen Victoria had written to her eldest daughter, Vicky, the Empress Frederick of Germany: 'It seems that it has never happened in this Country that there shd. be three direct Heirs as well as the Sovereign alive.' In her eagerness to greet the infant, the Queen travelled to White Lodge to lunch with his parents. On the way from Richmond Station to the Lodge itself she found herself heartily cheered by euphoric crowds thronging the narrow streets of the town. Then as now, however, royal births did not throw the entire population into fits of

Prince Edward, centre, with Princess Mary, left, and Prince Albert ('Bertie'), right, 1907

unbridled delight. By opposing a House of Commons motion that 'a humble address' of congratulations should be conveyed to the Queen, the radical politician Keir Hardie outraged Members of Parliament by delivering a prophecy that would, in time, prove devastatingly precise. This is what he said:

From his childhood onward, this boy will be surrounded by sycophants and flatterers by the score and will be taught to believe himself as of a superior creation. A line will be drawn between him and the people he is to be called upon some day to reign over. In due course, following the precedent which has already been set, he will be sent on a tour round the world and probably rumours of a morganatic alliance will follow . . . the end of it all will be that the country will be called upon to pay the bill.

Presentiments of disaster were far from mind as the Victorian public continued to bask in the steady glow of Britain's mighty achievements, and there was little to tarnish the lives of the young Duke and Duchess of York. Although the Duchess, like Queen Victoria before her, looked upon child-bearing with disdain, she nevertheless presented her husband with a second son, as well as a daughter, before the end of the 1890s – followed, in fairly brisk succession, by a further trio of boys. Prince Edward, or 'David' as he would always be known to his family, was eighteen months old when in December 1895 his brother 'Bertie', Prince Albert – the future King George VI – was born. Sixteen months later, in April 1897, the royal brothers were joined by their only sister 'Mary'. In March 1900 the Duchess of York gave birth to her third son, 'Harry' (Prince Henry, afterwards Duke of Gloucester); Prince George, later to become Duke of Kent, was born in December 1902; and the birth of Prince John, whom epilepsy would carry off to an early grave, followed in July 1905.

'Gan-Gan', Prince Edward's great-grandmother, Queen Victoria

Although no bigger than most Victorian or Edwardian families, and somewhat smaller than a great many more, the York tribe – plus sundry household attendants and servants – packed themselves into a house that was, even by middle-class standards, several sizes too small. Sometimes ambiguously described as being no bigger than a vicarage, York Cottage, on the Sandringham estate in Norfolk, was a warren of small, over-furnished rooms. It was a house in which every sound travelled through the thin walls, and where every room was pervaded by cooking smells seeping from the kitchen. All the same, the Duke of York, an unimaginative man at the best of times, adored it.

It was at York Cottage that Prince Edward spent much of what he subsequently called a 'wretched childhood'. Today, some maintain that, as Duke of Windsor, embittered by the treatment he received after his abdication, Prince Edward deluded himself into believing that his child-hood had been unhappy. Perhaps to some small extent this was so. But there would seem to be little evidence to support the belief that any of the York children rejoiced in a loving, caring atmosphere. Stories of practical jokes played on royal tutors, childish games, and other superficial goings-on are inadequate when put forward as being representative of childhood happiness in its entirety. Thus, since so much in life is judged in hindsight, we must allow Prince Edward's claim that, although 'there were short periods of happiness', he remembered his formative years 'chiefly for the miserableness' he had always had to keep to himself. We must also accept that his parents were largely to blame for the 'wretchedness' of it all.

Neither the Duke of York nor his wife, the former Princess Victoria Mary of Teck, were demonstrative or overtly affectionate individuals and, while it is perfectly true to say that theirs was a highly successful partnership, it is extremely difficult to believe that their feelings for one another were ever passionately expressed. It is hardly surprising to know, therefore, that 'Georgie' and 'May', as they were called, were depressingly ineffectual as parents.

Before long the Duke had assumed the guise of martinet: an insensitive, hectoring, bullish man of limited intellect, who embarrassed and repri-manded his sons with sufficient regularity for them to fear a summons to the Library, lest it should mean yet another dressing down for some misdemeanour, no matter how petty. Yet if the Duke failed to communi-cate with his offspring in a natural or affectionate manner, the Duchess herself was equally hopeless. Shy, aloof, and regally distant, ever aware of her position, she appeared totally devoid of maternal instincts. Indeed, she shared with her husband a marked inability to talk of intimate matters face to face, preferring instead to commit her feelings to paper. The Duke and Duchess thus exchanged innumerable letters through the years. Remarkably, 'May' even *wrote* to her husband about her feelings for their children; about her eldest son, when he was still a baby, she noted: 'I really believe he begins to like me at last, he is most civil to me.' From that sentence alone we not only gain some idea of the emotional obstacles that littered the Duchess's life, but something of the gulf that distanced her as a mother from her children.

In her biography of Edward VIII, Frances Donaldson wrote:

The earliest years are the most formative and during these years the most necessary part of a child's environment is his mother's love. Given the security of mother-love, the child will gradually and naturally be weaned from his dependence on it, whereas denied it, he may seek it in one form or another for the rest of his life. [The Duchess of York's] exceptionally reserved and undemonstrative temperament made it impossible for her to give her children the love and affection which is taken for granted in happier homes.

The gulf between royal mother and royal son is further accentuated in this case by the knowledge that the Duchess, much less the Duke, appeared never to question Prince Edward's tearful outbursts each time he was 'presented' to them by his nursemaid. Clearly the Duchess of York simply put her son's fractious behaviour down to 'incivility' and, once he was whisked back to his nursery, thought no more about it. In fact it was not until the Prince was three years old that his parents discovered that his nurse was an obsessive and unstable creature, and that the child's distress when in their presence was caused by the nursemaid's habit of pinching him or twisting his arm immediately before entering the room. The nurse was dismissed – but at what cost to Prince Edward and his brother 'Bertie', whose lifelong stomach trouble was almost certainly a legacy of his erratic feeding and general neglect while in the care of this unfortunate servant?

In the spring of 1902, by which time their grandfather, the eldest son of Queen Victoria, had at last ascended the throne as King Edward VII, and their parents had become Prince and Princess of Wales, Prince Edward, who was almost eight, and his brother 'Bertie', little more than six, found the feminine influence of the York Cottage nursery banished from their lives. Now they were entrusted to the care of Frederick Finch. At the age of thirty, this 'handsome, stalwart and muscular' footman, who was to remain in the elder prince's service for very many years, assumed the role of surrogate father, becoming all things to his royal charges – nurse, valet, confidant, confessor, referee, and hero.

There presently arrived at York Cottage one Henry Peter Hansell, employed by the new Prince of Wales as tutor to his sons. Appointed more or less on the strength of his Norfolk origins and his acknowledged ability as a yachtsman – wildly inappropriate credentials for any man about to educate not one but two future Kings of England – Hansell at least was aware of his own shortcomings, even if the Prince of Wales was not. In later life Prince Edward was to wonder if his tutor 'did not have a secret yearning for some other kind of life and whether he ever regretted having dedicated himself to the care and education of unwilling and ungrateful little boys'. Looking back on his youth, the Duke of Windsor was 'appalled to discover' how little he had learned from Henry Hansell and added that he was 'unable to recall anything brilliant or original that he ever said'. That aside, Hansell did his limited best to educate his royal pupils and in his mission he was assisted by three others. French and German (Prince Edward thought the former a feminine language, but became fluent in the latter) were taught by Monsieur Gabriel Hua and Professor Eugen Oswald respectively, while mathematics was the responsibility of a Mr Martin David, who had been recruited from Tonbridge School.

Light relief in the young Prince Edward's early life – doubtless included in the 'short periods of happiness' he later remembered – came in the form of his adoring, over-indulgent grandparents. As Prince and Princess of Wales, Edward VII and his Queen, the former Princess Alexandra of Denmark, had presided over the celebrated 'Marlborough House Set'. This was high society at its best (and sometimes its worst), a court apart from that ruled over by Queen Victoria. A large, jovial, bewhiskered man, with all the looks of his Hanoverian forebears, Edward VII, whose corpulence earned him the nickname 'Tum Tum', enjoyed his social life excessively. Yet he resented the long years spent as king-in-waiting, denied all dealings with matters of state, or indeed matters of any real purpose, by his mother, the Queen. Edward therefore whiled away his time by indulging in plutocratic pursuits, seeking little or no intellectual stimulation beyond what might generally be described as wine, women and song.

Throughout his life, the King had always had a particularly keen eye for the ladies. Among his most famous mistresses were 'Skittles' Walters, Daisy, Countess of Warwick, Lily Langtree, and Alice Keppel, and his

A doting grandfather: King Edward VII with 'David', 'Harry', Mary and 'Bertie'

paramours were all paraded before the long-suffering Queen Alexandra. Yet although she bore her husband's adulterous behaviour with infinite fortitude, it caused the ever-youthful Queen – said to have been England's most beautiful Queen ever – considerable unhappiness. As a measure of compensation, she mercilessly indulged her grandchildren, especially 'David' (Prince Edward), not only to their great delight, but to hers also.

Prince Edward's adored grandmother, Queen Alexandra

In 1901, Prince George and Princess May, then still Duke and Duchess of York, set out on a long tour of duty to Australia, while their children were consigned to the care of the King and Queen, up at 'the big house' – as Sandringham House itself was known to them – half a mile from York Cottage. There any notion of discipline was cast to the wind. The children were encouraged not only to run wild and show off to their hearts' content, but to mix freely with their grandparents' guests, often with amusing results. On one occasion, having recently shot an underweight stag in error, the royal physician, Sir Felix Semon, found himself asked by the young Prince Edward:

'Have you killed a little staggie today, Sir Felix?'

To Semon's reply, 'Who set you on this, Prince Eddie?' the little boy gleefully declared, 'Grandpapa' – a response that was doubtless greeted with a roar of laughter from the King himself.

Prince Edward at the age of eight. The first study of him on a pony, 1902

Despite his natural exuberance, there was already something about the boy 'David' that seemed to presage future events. In her biography Lady Donaldson reminds us of Lord Esher's first-hand observations of the Prince, during one of his visits to Windsor Castle. 'It was queer looking through a weekly paper and coming to [his] picture with the label "our future King",' Esher noted. 'Prince Albert at once drew attention to it – but the elder hastily brushed his brother's fingers away and turned the page.' And again: 'Prince Edward develops every day fresh qualities, and is a most charming boy; very direct, dignified and clever. His memory is remarkable – a family tradition; but the look of *Weltschmerz* [world-weariness] in his eyes I cannot trace to any ancestor of the House of Hanover.' Lady Donaldson commented: 'From what Lord Esher tells us, although [the Prince] had the fairest looks, he had quite early acquired an air of wistfulness, as though something in the view from his elevated position had permanently blighted his hopes.'

Prince Edward, his sister and brothers at Balmoral with their tutor, Monsieur Hua

Whatever Prince Edward's view, as seen from his royally 'elevated position', the immediate future held in prospect a further change of regimen, dictated once more by his father. This was to prove decidedly colder than anything he had known at York Cottage.

In September 1877, when he was a boy of twelve, Edward's father, the future George V, and his backward and unmanly elder brother Albert Victor had been allowed to join the Royal Navy's training ship *Britannia*, on the river Dart in Devon. Yet while Prince George enjoyed himself, as an 'experiment' in educating a future King it was hardly successful, and the results were far from satisfactory. Nevertheless, in the curiously narrow belief that the Royal Navy would teach his elder sons all they would need to know, the Prince of Wales arranged for 'David' and then 'Bertie' to take the entrance exams that would precede the admission of both boys, in turn, to the Royal Naval College, Osborne.

So it was that in the spring of 1907, one month before his thirteenth birthday, Prince Edward bade farewell to his family. Proudly dressed in his dark blue uniform jacket, 'with its brass buttons and cadet's white collar tab', as the Duke of Windsor wrote in his memoirs, but with tears streaming down his face, the young Prince left his parents' London home, by now Marlborough House, the former residence of his grandparents, for Portsmouth. From there he went by Admiralty yacht to Cowes on the Isle of Wight and the Royal Naval College itself, which occupied a site in the grounds of Osborne House, Queen Victoria's beloved Italianate villa. Prince Edward was accompanied on the journey by his father, who in kindly manner told him, 'Now that you are leaving home, David, and going out into the world, always remember that I am your best friend.' The Prince of Wales had always regarded his own father in exactly that light; but for Prince Edward such an exhortation, no matter how sincere, was hard to swallow. Best friends father and son would never be.

✱

Nothing but a proper school education in the company of other boys could have helped prepare Prince Edward for the rigours of Osborne. At the Royal Naval College, with its strict discipline, spartan accommodation, and frequently inedible food, the Prince had to share a dormitory with thirty other boys and, like them, had to adjust to a routine that made life at York Cottage seem like heaven in comparison.

With reveille at 6 a.m. – half an hour later in winter – the boys were

Naval cadet and the Lord High Admiral Prince Edward with his father, King George V

expected to snap to life and at the double, as everything had to be done at Osborne: jump from their beds, say their prayers, brush their teeth, and, to the accompaniment of a gong that timed each phase of their morning ritual, race to the end of the dormitory where a douse in cold water most assuredly roused the cadets for the day ahead. In his memoirs, published over forty years later, the Duke of Windsor recalled: 'Today I have only to close my eyes to see again that pathetic crowd of naked, shivering little boys, myself among them, being herded reluctantly towards that green-tiled pool in the first morning light.'

Until 'lights out', many long hours away, the cadets worked to a rigid curriculum set out by the Admiralty, with special emphasis on science, navigation, engineering, and mathematics (a subject in which neither Prince Edward nor Prince Albert excelled). They learned to 'tie knots and splice rope, sail a cutter, read and make signals, box the compass, and master all the intricacies of seamanship'. At the end of each term came the examinations and the inevitable term report, which apprised each of the cadets' parents of their son's achievements and failures.

Having heard no word of complaint from the Prince of Wales about his first report, Prince Edward took the second one home to York Cottage, believing it to be no worse. Alas, he was mistaken, and he duly received the dreaded summons to his father's Library. 'My father looked me in the eye. "David," he said, "I am sorry to have to tell you that you have a bad report. Read it!" ' That the paper told a different story from that which Prince Edward had anticipated was in itself sufficient reprimand. But when, at the end of the boy's third term, the Prince of Wales again beckoned from his Library, Prince Edward burst into tears before his father had opened his mouth. To his astonishment, the Prince was not about to issue yet another admonition, and, having told his son to dry his tears, murmuring, 'Come, David, this is no way for a naval cadet to act', went on to say that he was pleased with the progress Edward had made. Progress was, however, something of a moot point where Prince Edward and his brother were concerned, particularly since neither ever managed to move much above bottom of the class. Despite his sons' attempts to excuse their disappointing results, the Prince of Wales's reaction remained as predictable as ever. In later life Prince Edward was often to remark upon the extreme difficulties of trying to explain to his father that poor results were not indicative of sloth or stupidity, but simply that Hansell, the York Cottage tutor, had not taught 'Bertie' or himself very much. Nor, judging by the fact that Prince Edward had to spend part of his holidays taking extra tuition in maths, had Mr David the mathematician.

In May 1909, two years after being admitted to Osborne, the cadet Prince graduated to the senior Royal Naval College at Dartmouth, there to complete the final two years of his naval training. Of the two academies, Prince Edward preferred Dartmouth, with its improvements in appearance

(an imposing red-brick building overlooking the river Dart), more comfortable accommodation and better amenities, better food – including cream teas on Sundays – and a greater measure of freedom. There were, for example, Saturday-night dances in the central hall, or the 'Quarter Deck', as it was known. Yet while the senior college offered a little more than Osborne by way of creature comforts, the required standards of work, discipline, and achievement were no less stringent. Even the wicked ragging devised for, and bravely endured by, the younger cadets, or 'warts', seemed more sophisticated. At Osborne red ink had been poured over Prince Edward's blond head, and his neck had been 'guillotined' by a sash window. At Dartmouth the term's cadet captain thought up something infinitely more dastardly. Upbraiding the cadets for being an idle and lazy bunch who needed 'a good shake-up', he decreed that they no longer had the regulation one minute in which to undress, put on pyjamas, and get to the washroom each evening, but thirty seconds. Even to these boys, by now well accustomed to obeying instructions and doing everything at the double, this was a horribly tall order and one that called for a bit of ingenious cheating, if a thrashing after 'lights out' was to be avoided. Inevitably some of the cadets failed to meet the deadline and were accordingly punished, but the majority evidently managed to comply with the order by removing such things as undergarments before falling in for evening prayers in the central hall. Afterwards, however, the ensuing rush to the dormitory truly was a case of every man for himself.

In the Duke of Windsor's own words once more: 'No one watching us marching out . . . could have guessed the ordeal ahead. For, as soon as we were through the big doors, a stampede began. We tripped in the passage and fell up the stairs in our frantic struggles to reach the dormitory and get undressed and pass the cadet captain, standing by, watch in hand under the gun.' Only when word finally reached the Term Lieutenant two or three weeks later was his subordinate's order revoked, and at least one of the cadets' nightmares was laid to rest.

*

In May 1910, Easter leave for Prince Edward and his brother Prince Albert (who had joined the ranks of naval cadets at Osborne sixteen months earlier) was unexpectedly protracted by the death of their grandfather.

Edward VII, already fifty-nine by the time he ascended the throne, had not always been a popular figure either within the royal family or with the

In a chair lift aboard ship;
an informal photograph of
the young Prince Edward

Prince Edward at Dartmouth, 1909

nation at large. But by the end of his reign of only nine years he had earned his people's respect and admiration, together with the sobriquet 'Edward the Peacemaker'. Indeed, had he lived longer he might well have made an even greater impression on international affairs. Be that as it may, Edward VII was responsible for a very significant change in British foreign policy, namely the *Entente Cordiale* with France. He had also established other foreign alliances and had begun active rearmament against Germany's military aggrandizement under the Kaiser – his own detested nephew, Wilhelm II.

The King's death occurred at Buckingham Palace shortly before midnight on Friday 6 May 1910. That afternoon his filly Witch of the Air had won the 4.15 at Kempton Park, and it was this news that George, Prince of Wales, was able to impart to his father shortly before he died.

During the small hours of 7 May, the new King George V wrote in his diary: 'At 11.45 beloved Papa passed peacefully away and I have lost my best friend and the best of fathers. I am heartbroken and overwhelmed with grief.' Later that morning, 'David' and 'Bertie' were told of their grandfather's demise. Prince Edward replied that, from the windows of the bedroom they shared at Marlborough House, he and Prince Albert had already seen the Royal Standard flying at half-mast over Buckingham Palace. Taking in this serious breach of royal protocol (the Standard is never lowered in tribute, not even on the sovereign's death), their weeping father muttered repeatedly to himself, 'But that's all wrong . . . The King is Dead. Long live the King,' and within the hour the sovereign's banner had been raised over Marlborough House.

The funeral of Edward VII took place at St George's Chapel, Windsor Castle, on 20 May. While their mother – now Queen Mary – rode in a carriage, as did the other heavily veiled royal ladies, the Princes Edward and Albert joined their uniformed kinsmen following the King's coffin on foot. Although the Princes had witnessed the funeral of Queen Victoria at Windsor, on a bitingly cold day nine years earlier, that of their grandfather represented the first of the many state ceremonials in which they were destined to play conspicuous roles.

Three weeks into the new reign, Prince Edward was permitted to return to Dartmouth, no longer the grandson of a King but Heir Apparent in his own right. No sooner had the Prince resumed his studies, however, than he was recalled to Windsor. George V had decided to create his son and heir Prince of Wales. From this point on, the tone of Prince Edward's life

changed completely. To his great dismay his career at the Royal Naval
College was brought to an abrupt and premature end. For him there would
be no final training cruise to North America and no formal graduation
from Dartmouth. The 'goal' of his cadet life, his 'first serious ambition', as
he put it, had been unhappily thwarted. The demands imposed by his
newly bestowed rank – and the restrictive demands of his royal heritage –
meant that, at seventeen, Prince Edward had already come of age.

– 2 –

PRINCE OF WALES

FOR PRINCE EDWARD, as indeed for the King and Queen, the summer of 1911 was made unforgettable by a sequence of events that would pass their way but once. At Windsor Castle on 10 June, in a ceremony of medieval splendour that seemed scarcely to have changed since its inception in 1348, King George V formally admitted his eldest son to the Most Noble Order of the Garter, England's most ancient order of chivalry.

Twelve days later, wearing his Garter robe of deep blue velvet over a costume made from cloth-of-silver, the Prince knelt at the King's throne in Westminster Abbey, during the equally ancient coronation ritual, and paid homage to his father with the time-honoured words, 'I, Edward, Prince of Wales, do become your liege man of life and limb, and of earthly worship; and faith and truth I will bear unto you, to live and die, against all manner of folks. So help me God.' For both the King and his son, this was a particularly moving moment in what has always been the most stirring, as well as the single most significant, of all royal ceremonies.

Prince Edward noted in his diary that day: 'When my father kissed my cheeks, his emotion was great, as was mine.' In his diary, the King wrote: 'I nearly broke down when dear David came to do homage to me, as it reminded me so much of when I did the same thing to beloved Papa, he did it so well.'

'Coronation fever' that summer continued undiminished as the King and Queen, Prince Edward, and Princess Mary set out on a royal progress throughout Britain. On 14 July public euphoria reached a new high when, at the conclusion of the royal family's visit to Wales, the people of the principality witnessed the Investiture of the Heir Apparent at Caernarvon Castle.

The honour and dignity of the rank he had so lately come to hold, and the meaning of the Investiture itself, were not lost on the Prince for a single moment. Yet amid all the pomp and magnificence of the occasion, Edward

The twentieth Prince of Wales: Prince Edward dressed in his 'preposterous rig', 1911

was startled by what he called 'a painful discovery' about himself. The Prince's feelings of inner conflict were evidently precipitated by an issue of relative unimportance. In his own words:

The ceremony I had to go through with, the speech I had to make, and the Welsh I had to speak were, I thought, a sufficient ordeal for anyone. But when a tailor appeared to measure me for a fantastic costume . . . of white satin breeches and a mantle and surcoat of purple velvet edged with ermine, I decided things had gone too far. I had already submitted to the Garter dress . . . for which there existed a condoning historical precedent; but what would my Navy friends say if they saw me in this preposterous rig?

A Knight of the Garter. The Prince walking in procession with the King of Portugal, left, and the Duke of Connaught

Queen Mary managed to soothe her son's understandable indignation over the pantomime garb that had been designed for him. And, on the day itself, the warmth of the response he received from the eleven thousand spectators packed within the ruined walls of Caernarvon Castle, and the cheers of all those who thronged the streets outside, may conceivably have eclipsed his feelings of embarrassment. But from that one incident, the young Prince of Wales, as he was to recall in his memoirs, began to recoil from anything that tended to set him up as a 'person requiring homage'. He went on:

> even if my father was now beginning to remind me of the obligations of my position, had he not been at pains to give me a strict and unaffected upbringing? And if my association with the village boys at Sandringham and the cadets of the Naval Colleges had done anything for me, it was to make me desperately anxious to be treated exactly like any other boy of my age.

Refreshing though Prince Edward's feelings may seem to us today, the chances that he – or any royal figure – could ever be treated in the same way as lesser mortals, even as his upper-class contemporaries, were non-existent. At birth he had become the captive of a system, ruled by what is generally referred to as 'the Establishment', which demanded total obedience of its princes and princesses. For unquestioning devotion to the monarchic idyll, the material rewards and privileges were incalculable, but the royal world would always be a world apart. If homage belonged anywhere, therefore, it belonged at the very apex of a system that Prince Edward was destined to represent as King and which, yet more significantly, he would one day challenge. It is ironic, however, that despite his earlier ambivalence, homage was one of the trappings of royalty which the Prince, as Duke of Windsor, came to insist upon in the wilderness that was his from the day he abdicated to the day he died.

In her book *The Royal House of Windsor*, Elizabeth Longford gave a wider interpretation of the acts which the then Prince of Wales found so abhorrent. 'Homage', she wrote, 'was not being paid to one sort of "person" or another . . . but to the ancient institution of monarchy. No one was abased; the monarchy was honoured . . . in a manner hallowed by history. Taken out of its historic context, the act would be meaningless if not repellent.' In short, Lady Longford concluded, the Prince of Wales 'had failed to distinguish between the person and the office'. Again, one wonders if a better education might not have given Prince Edward a deeper understanding of such matters. At all events, the Investiture at Caernarvon had aroused the rebel in the young Prince and had set him on a course that would inevitably result in a head-on collision with Establishment forces.

In 1911 George V sought to quell his son's rising emotions by arranging for him to go to sea as a midshipman aboard the Royal Navy's battleship *Hindustan*. Here at least was some recompense for the training voyage his unexpected elevation had deprived him of at Dartmouth. Yet even so, in the rather pointless way royal menfolk have so often had of becoming briefly attached to the armed services — and ultimately discovering themselves promoted to exalted rank for achieving precious little — the Prince of Wales's renewed flirtation with the Navy was a short-lived affair lasting no more than three months.

The King, who now declared a career at sea to be 'too specialized', had decided upon a three-point plan for his son's further education. In the Library at York Cottage, to which he had once more been summoned, the Prince listened as his father outlined his new stratagem. The first point was that Prince Edward must give up the Navy. Second, the Prince was to undertake trips to France and Germany in order to learn the languages and the politics of those countries. Third, Prince Edward was to go up to Oxford University. At this the Prince remonstrated with his father that, since he had 'neither the mind nor the will for books', the experience would be lost on him. Would it not be better, he argued, for him to be sent on a world tour? That way he could learn about people and places at first hand. The King would have none of it. His mind was made up; or at least, it had been made up for him by Mr Hansell, who had been kept on at York Cottage to teach Prince Edward's younger brothers. Hansell's intellectual capabilities, as we have already seen, were limited, but it is still remarkable that the one man who should have realized the shortcomings of his former pupil, as no other, should have suggested the Oxford idea to the King. Be that as it may, the decision had been taken, and now George V set about looking for suitable companions for his son during his time at university.

Lord Derby, an old friend of the King, was among those approached. His written response — sheer poetry in terms of obsequious gratitude — tells us much, not only about the attitudes of those who surrounded the King and who thus revelled in royal favour but also, alas, about the awful snobbery that is still one of the most flourishing and least attractive features of English society. In part, Lord Derby wrote:

Left The student Prince at Oxford

Right The Prince of Wales in Paris with his tutor, Henry Hansell, 1912

Mr Hansell has been to see me and tells me Your Majesty would like my eldest boy to go to the same college as H.R.H. The Prince of Wales. I cannot say how pleased and honoured I am and how gladly I will consent to his going to whatever college is chosen.

There appear to be three in the running – Christ Church, New and Magdalen. New College I should not like as according to the Archbishop of York there is much trouble there and his is a judgement I would implicitly rely on. Christ Church is a large college where all the *nouveaux riches* go . . . Magdalen would appear to have none of these disadvantages, and if Your Majesty chooses this college I can only most humbly say I should be very content . . . May I again say how honoured I am by Your Majesty's wish and how much I hope that Edward may be as devoted to the Prince of Wales as I am to Your Majesty.

Magdalen did in fact win the royal accolade, but as it was Henry Hansell's old college it isn't altogether surprising. At that time Oxford had a popular reputation for being less 'snooty' than Cambridge. Yet even here the Prince, who yearned for equality, would need to have been blind not to notice that his rooms in 'cloisters' had been newly decorated, or that he was the first undergraduate to be allowed the privilege of a private bathroom.

Described as having been 'diffident and lonely' when he first arrived at Magdalen, the Prince of Wales soon established himself as an extremely popular figure. Having shunned the company of the public-schoolboy types, at least to begin with, he was admired for his modesty in choosing friends. These things aside, however, the Prince was manifestly *un*suited to

A formal portrait of the Prince of Wales at the age of twenty

university life. It is true that he enjoyed what he saw of it; he often spoke fondly about his days at Oxford, particularly in later years, and was always keen to have the latest news from Magdalen. But his personal preferences for hunting and polo overrode the reasons for his being sent to Oxford in the first place. Yet, when faced with a secure and all too predictable future, what real need has any prince of an honours degree? Summing up Prince Edward's eight 'agreeable but desultory terms' at Oxford, Kenneth Rose tells us: 'The Prince joined the Officer's Training Corps, played football, got drunk, was introduced to constitutional law by Sir William Anson and to fox-hunting by an equerry.'

Even Sir Herbert Warren, President of Magdalen and 'a man too much remembered for his social pretensions, too little for his classical scholarship and love of letters', had to concede of his most illustrious undergraduate: 'Bookish he will never be.' This was a line that the Prince himself frequently enjoyed repeating to the end of his life and, equally, because it has been quoted so often, was one that earned the distinction of being the most famous extract of a report Sir Herbert Warren had put together after the Prince of Wales left Oxford.

Originally published in *The Times* at the end of 1914, the full report provides a glowing account of a young man whose charm and lack of 'side' were soon to endear him to untold millions. 'From the first', the President of Magdalen wrote, the Prince

took his own line, with equal modesty and firmness, determined in his own mind that he would be really *par inter pares*, that he would seek and accept no tribute except on his merits, that he would take as habitual and as assiduous trouble to avoid deference and preference as others to cultivate it, desiring as the old Roman poet put it, 'that men should give what they wanted, but that they should be free to deny'. . . . His natural dignity and charm, and it should be added, the good sense and feeling of his college companions, and of Oxford generally . . . enabled him to go far in this resolve without mishap or untoward result. Once having started on it he pursued this narrow, nice line with increased confidence until it seemed the most easy and natural and unconscious thing in the world.

*

When the Prince returned to London from Oxford in June 1914, he found himself briefly attached to the 1st Life Guards for no other purpose than to improve his seat on a horse. Once more the initiative had been taken by

Colonel of the Welsh
Guards. A formal study

George V. Agitated by his son's unsatisfactory appearance on horseback, the King was at pains to point out that if the prince couldn't ride properly – and it was imperative for him to do so – people would call him a 'duffer'. The outcome was a month's riding instruction which occupied two hours every morning and found the Prince of Wales, along with a number of recruits, enduring mounted sword drill, bareback riding, fence jumping, and any other exercise included in the Household Cavalry's bone-jarring training programme.

Hard work though his morning sessions at the riding school were, the Prince seemed none the worse for them; nor, indeed, did the early start they demanded prevent him from enjoying the fruits of the season. At the age of twenty Prince Edward, so he tells us, was growing up, and in finding a new confidence in himself he had begun to shake off some of his earlier inhibitions.

From his first high-society ball in the capital, given by Lord and Lady Londesborough on 7 July, he arrived back at Buckingham Palace at 2 a.m. From a ball given by the Duke of Portland the following evening the Prince arrived home later still, this time at 4 a.m. So intoxicated was he by the social whirl – 'I have now become fond of dancing & love going out!!' – that on 10 July he proudly confessed to his diary: 'I've had no more than 8 hrs. sleep in the last 72 hrs.!!' In the meantime, beyond the giddy round of parties for Britain's giddy young grandees, the ominous roll of events that would snuff out more than the shimmering chandeliers of London's fine houses was gaining momentum. On 4 August 1914 the world was at war, and the Prince of Wales asked for, and was granted, a commission in the Grenadier Guards.

On being gazetted, the Prince was posted to the 1st Battalion, stationed at Warley Barracks in Brentwood, Essex, and, although he failed to meet the required height of 6 feet (the prince maintained he was 5 feet 7 inches, while others have put him at 5 feet 4, the same height as his grandfather, Edward VII) he was overjoyed to be detailed to the King's Company. Then followed the strenuous training that any soldier knows: route marches, field exercises, rifle practice, and so on, all of which lasted for ten days before the 1st Battalion Grenadier Guards was moved to London and quartered in greater comfort at Wellington Barracks on Birdcage Walk, within sight of Buckingham Palace.

Prince Edward's pleasure at being commissioned into the Guards was soon marred, however, when he was suddenly transferred to the 3rd

Battalion and, after forty-eight hours' leave – taken as a sure sign that the Guards were to be posted overseas – was returned to Brentwood. Attempting to mask his bitter disappointment, the Prince visited his father and asked him why he was to be left behind. The King replied that the decision had not been his and passed the buck to the Secretary of State for War, Lord Kitchener. Princes at war, Edward discovered, were treated pretty much the same as Princes at peace: a protected species. To his everlasting credit, Edward, Prince of Wales, could not accept the role of puppet prince – pretty and decorative when the occasion demanded, but otherwise kept well out of range. Thus, having secured an interview with Lord Kitchener, he registered his complaint at not being allowed to go with his battalion to France and insisted that, since he had four younger brothers, it would not much matter if he were to be killed. It was a brave argument, but one which Kitchener capped.

'If I were sure you would be killed,' he told Prince Edward, 'I do not know if I should be right to restrain you. But I cannot take the chance . . . of the enemy taking you prisoner.'

By the end of the year the Prince's persistent requests to be allowed to go to France had paid off, but to his chagrin he discovered that nothing more risky than a desk job on the staff of Field-Marshal Sir John French, Commander-in-Chief of the British Expeditionary Force, awaited him. Never more determined to battle his way through the barricades of bureaucracy that prevented him from taking an active part in the war, the Prince of Wales stepped up his badgering until, little by little, he started to gain ground. In May 1915 he was attached to the General Staff of the 1st Army Corps, stationed near Bethune, no more than five miles from the front line. Although the Prince – despite his constant harassment of anybody who might help further his cause – would never be allowed to fight in the trenches, he could at least see for himself what was happening at the front and never missed an opportunity to do so. Then, in September 1915, he was appointed to the staff of Major-General Lord Cavan, commanding the newly formed Guards Division, whom he accompanied on a near-fatal tour of the divisional front-line sector before Loos on 29 September.

That day the Prince of Wales and Lord Cavan had driven to the ruined village of Vermelles, from where they proceeded on foot to the Guards' Headquarters, occupying the ruins of a nearby farm. Heavy shelling presently forced them down into the muddy, body-strewn trenches for the

rest of their progress. From the farm itself, they crawled and climbed towards an observation station, affording the Prince 'some idea of the horror & ghastliness of it all!!' Upon their return to Vermelles, Prince Edward and Lord Cavan emerged from the trenches – which the Prince described as a 'continuous wallow in a foot of mud the whole way' – to discover their car peppered with bullet holes and their driver dead, shot through the heart. 'I can't yet realise that it has happened,' the Prince noted in his diary that evening, then added: 'I have seen and learnt a lot about war today.'

Shocked though Prince Edward undoubtedly was, that potential brush with death did not unnerve him in any way. It did unnerve Sir John French, however, who immediately ordered the King's son to be transferred to the safety of XI Corps Staff. Ever alert, the Prince himself acted before Sir John's instructions could be implemented and when he met the Commander-in-Chief managed to persuade him to rescind the order.

Even the King, who was constantly apprised of his son's bravery and dogged determination to be of real assistance, readily understood the Prince's need to be in the front line, and assured Lord Cavan that neither he nor any other officer was to be held responsible for the younger man's safety. Yet even now, in the very midst of the Great War, the views of the King and the Prince of Wales were to clash, this time over the question of decorations. To the Prince, wearing medals or ribbons that he had not been given the opportunity of earning was deeply distasteful. The King on the other hand insisted that he must wear the Légion d'honneur (presented to him by the French, albeit in peacetime) together with 'the Russian orders' bestowed on him by his father's cousin, Tsar Nicholas II, lest their absence should give offence. The Prince replied that, since he hadn't done any fighting and had been kept out of danger, he felt ashamed to wear medals that had been awarded simply because of his position as heir to the throne. His shame was further compounded, as he told his father, by the fact that there were thousands of gallant men, all leading the most wretched lives in the trenches, who had not been decorated.

It was this agreeable spirit, so entirely refreshing in a member of the royal family, that endeared the Prince of Wales to the ordinary soldier. To the majority it mattered little that he wasn't there in the trenches fighting alongside them. What was important was that he *wanted* to be. Even more to the point, the men knew that Prince Edward understood what they endured, that he had witnessed the devastation and horror of war, the

France, 1918. The Prince of Wales talking informally with the troops

squalor of the trenches, with his own eyes and, like them, had learned to fear and loathe all that war represented.

✳

In the spring of 1916 the Prince of Wales was dispatched from France on a six-week visit to the Middle East, the object of his mission being to inspect defences on the Suez Canal and to report his findings. It was a job the Prince welcomed, if only because it afforded him the opportunity of working in a different area of military operations and, as he later put it, of getting to know 'the magnificent Australian and New Zealand troops – the Anzacs – who had recently been evacuated from Gallipoli'. From the Middle East the Prince returned to France, reporting for duty with XIV Army Corps at Ypres. Two months later XIV Corps was ordered to the Somme, where Prince Edward lamented: 'Oh! to be fighting with those grand fellows & not sitting back here doing so little as compared to them

With General the Earl of Cavan on the Italian Front, 1917

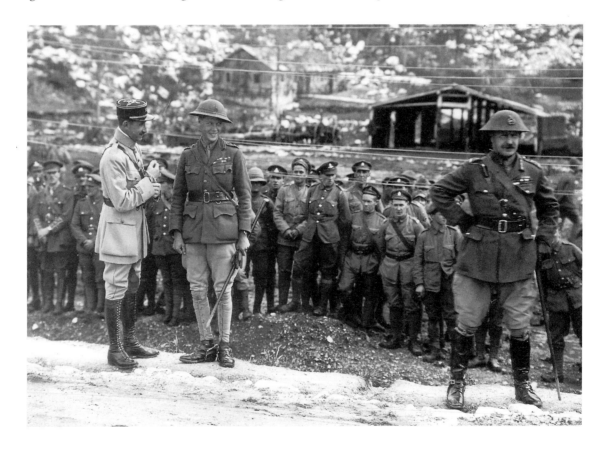

who are sacrificing their lives!! There could be no finer death & if one was spared how proud one would feel to have been thro it.' Already sickened by the mass carnage and the nauseating destruction of life that he saw everywhere, it was not until the advent of the Battle of Passchendaele (July to November 1917) that the Prince got what he called 'the most vivid close-ups of the horrible existence that had become the lot of the British soldier'.

In the autumn of 1917, XIV Army Corps – and with it the Prince of Wales – was ordered to Italy, to 'bolster' the retreat of the Italian army from Caporetto. The Prince remained there until March 1918 when he was sent back to England for six weeks to make a tour of defence plants. When he returned to France, Prince Edward received a posting from Lord Cavan's XIV Army Corps to the staff of the Canadian Corps, and there he remained until the war's end. With the Armistice of 11 November 1918 the Prince of Wales did not return immediately to London but, as part of the Australian Corps stationed in Belgium, visited the occupation troops in Germany and there made contact for the first time with the American Expeditionary Force, an experience which, among other things, introduced him to 'crap-shooting'.

In February 1919, three months after the cessation of hostilities, Prince Edward, who always regarded himself, somewhat unnecessarily, as an 'insignificant staff officer', was back home with his family, sharing an emotion common to all survivors of war. 'Life', he wrote later, 'had never appeared more desirable, and everything I did seemed invested with a sort of magical charm.'

AMBASSADOR ROYAL

WITH HIS SLIGHT BUILD, blond hair, and blue eyes, Edward, Prince of Wales, was indisputably the best looking of King George V and Queen Mary's six children. He was also blessed with enormous charm and personality which, with the exception of his brother, Prince George, Duke of Kent, who ran a very near second, conspicuously passed his siblings by. Exceptionally good-looking as a boy, Prince Edward became a strikingly handsome young man, possessed of a 'Peter Pan' aura and a wistful, even sad, look in his eyes. Indeed, even when quite elderly and very much the *grand seigneur*, those characteristics remained evident.

Romantic though the Prince of Wales's image was, he was never to become the royal Lothario some of his friends loyally claimed him to be. The lie to his reputation as a passionate lover, with 'a girl in every port', is given by the knowledge that, until he married Wallis Simpson, his successes in that direction were negligible. There were nevertheless early signs of that particular quirk in the Prince's make-up that helped to lead to his downfall: in short, a marked preference for the society of married women. By the age of twenty-four, Prince Edward had put behind him a three-year relationship with the then Earl of Leicester's daughter-in-law, Viscountess Coke, who was the Prince's senior by twelve years. Commenting on the royal predilection, Lady Alexandra Metcalfe, one of the Prince of Wales's closest friends, said: 'The Prince always liked the company of married women and their sophisticated ways. He really wasn't very interested in girls of his own age.' There were, however, two exceptions to that rule; one purely platonic, the other a fleeting romance, seen at the end of the day as nothing more than a mild flirtation. The former was the almost lifelong friendship enjoyed with Lady Alexandra Metcalfe herself, the youngest

The Prince in Nova Scotia, 1919. Said to have been the Duchess of Windsor's favourite photograph of her husband

daughter of the Marquess Curzon of Kedleston and a god-daughter of the Prince's adored grandmother, Queen Alexandra.

The latter took the form of the Prince of Wales's romantic involvement with the Duke of Sutherland's daughter, Lady Rosemary Leveson-Gower. Popular legend has it that the Prince had considered marrying the Lady Rosemary, but that he was under the illusion that, to win the King's approval, he was expected to choose a royal princess (Frederike of Hanover, who eventually became the Queen of the Hellenes, was one such princess who was considered eligible). This particular notion is totally without foundation and, indeed, would seem too far-fetched. For, as early as 1917, King George V had told the Privy Council that he would not object to his children marrying into Britain's aristocratic families. Clearly, therefore, the Prince of Wales did not seriously contemplate marriage with Rosemary Leveson-Gower, or with anybody else at that time. At all events, the Earl of Dudley's son and heir, Viscount Ednam, won Lady Rosemary's hand, and they were married in 1919. As a friend of the family, the path of Prince Edward crossed regularly with that of the new Lady Ednam and would continue to do so in future. But whatever the Prince felt for the young Viscountess was entirely eclipsed by the presence in his life of the one woman he would prize above all others for very nearly twenty years. She was Mrs William Dudley Ward, whose husband was not only Liberal Member of Parliament for Southampton, but Vice-Chamberlain of the Royal Household.

Winifred Dudley Ward, or 'Freda' as she was better known, was the daughter of Colonel Charles Birkin, a well-to-do lace manufacturer, and his American wife Claire. A year younger than the Prince of Wales, Freda was twenty-three and had been married for five years when a chance encounter changed the pattern of her life – and his. They met one evening early in 1918 when Prince Edward attended a party at the home of Maud Kerr-Smiley in fashionable Belgravia. The demands a political career placed on her husband meant that Mrs Dudley Ward frequently organized her own entertainment, and on the night in question she and her escort were crossing Belgrave Square when the air-raid warnings began to sound, sending them scuttling towards the open door of the Kerr-Smiley house. When the party-goers became aware of the maroons, forerunners of the sirens that wailed out over London little more than twenty years later, they began filing downstairs, led by their hostess.

Unexpected guests though Freda and her companion were, Mrs Kerr-

Smiley invited them to shelter in the cellar. It was there, in that barely lit place, that a young man engaged Mrs Dudley Ward in small talk. When the all-clear sounded, Mrs Kerr-Smiley invited her new guests to join the party, adding, 'His Royal Highness is so anxious that you should do so.' The fates were evidently in mischievous mood. Not only did they direct Freda Dudley Ward into the arms of her future King that night, but they ensured that she should captivate him beneath the roof of a woman whose brother was the same Ernest Simpson who, ten years hence, would marry an American divorcee by the name of Wallis Spencer.

✳

In an era noted for its pretensions, Freda Dudley Ward managed to remain perfectly natural. Petite, gifted, and unaffectedly charming, she was generally considered to be one of the most attractive women of her generation, both in looks and in manner. From the highest to the lowest,

Left Freda Dudley Ward

Right The 'Golden' Prince of Empire

Mrs Dudley Ward treated everyone with the same courtesy and charming consideration; more than could be said for many of her contemporaries, royal or otherwise. Indeed, in time to come, she who was to be the mainstay of the Prince of Wales's life for a total of sixteen years, and who would be a gentle but wise and positive influence on an often petulant character, would feel the sting of being dismissed in the most cowardly fashion by the Prince. Before the advent of Mrs Simpson, however, Edward once went so far as to confess to his father that Freda Dudley Ward was the only woman he had really loved. In return King George V, to whom his son's mistress would never be an acceptable member of the Court circle, facetiously referred to Freda as 'the lacemaker's daughter'.

Prince Edward's relationship with his father, as tense and intimidating as it had always been, never matured. The King heartily disapproved of the modern, trend-setting way in which his son dressed; he despised his circle of friends. Given the dynastic hopes invested in the Heir Apparent, the Prince's fondness of other men's wives was, not unnaturally, another source of disappointment. So badly did father and son clash on one memorable occasion that a courtier overheard the King bellow at the Prince of Wales, 'You dress like a cad. You act like a cad. You *are* a cad. Get out!'

Of all his sons, George V recognized himself only in Prince Albert, a young man seriously afflicted by a speech impediment, in whom the frustrations of childhood became manifest in fits of uncontrollable rage, and upon whom the full responsibility of sovereignty would eventually fall. Only with 'Bertie' did the King manage to strike up anything approaching a warm rapport. Otherwise fear was the predominant emotion experienced by the royal princes in their dealings with their father. Freda Dudley Ward herself provided evidence of this. Speaking of the King's third son, Prince Henry – known to his family as 'Harry' and to certain others, for some obscure reason, as 'Potty' – she recalled something that happened when the Prince 'would have been about nineteen'. One night, she said,

he crept out of the Palace . . . with his dancing shoes in his hand and crept back again around five in the morning. A courtier saw him, and Harry knew he'd be reported to the King. It was an absolutely *unbreakable* rule that the boys came down to breakfast at five to nine and stood around until their father came down exactly as Big Ben began striking the hour. Then they all sat. Well, this particular morning, Harry was a few minutes late. When he came in, his father just *looked* at him – and Harry *fainted*. Imagine it, at *nineteen years old!*

That incident, amusing as it is to us, undoubtedly amused the Prince of Wales too, for there was never any love lost between Prince Henry and himself, something he made clear many years later in conversation with the beautiful actress Lilli Palmer. By this time 'Harry' had become Duke of

Gloucester, and Prince Edward was Duke of Windsor. He happened to ask Miss Palmer if she knew his brother 'Gloucester'.

'No, Sir,' she replied. 'I've never had the pleasure.'

'Pleasure!' groaned the Duke of Windsor, throwing his eyes to the ceiling. Then he asked, 'Did you know my brother Kent?'

'Unfortunately not.'

'Pity,' said the Duke. 'He was a fine chap.'

It was with Prince George, Duke of Kent, tragically killed in a flying accident with the Royal Air Force in August 1942, that the Prince of Wales shared an especially close relationship. Although Prince George was eight years younger, he and his brother were, in many ways, kindred spirits.

The epitome of style; the Prince of Wales leaving Lloyds in the City of London, followed by his brother Albert, the Duke of York

If the trappings of his Investiture at Caernarvon in the summer of 1911 had aroused the rebel in the Prince of Wales, the lack of warmth and understanding between the King and himself served only to exacerbate the unhappiness of the situation. Still the Prince could not reconcile himself to the kind of life his father would have wished him to lead, and the restrictions placed on those of royal birth continued to rankle. It was to Freda Dudley Ward, therefore, that the 'Little Prince' (as her daughters Penelope and Angela affectionately referred to him) ran to pour out his troubles.

An idea of the Prince's feelings about his royal life at this time is given by the American writers J. Bryan III and Charles J. V. Murphy in their book *The Windsor Story*. Mrs Dudley Ward, they tell us, remembered that King George V humiliated his eldest son

to the point where he actually burst into tears. I tried to put some stuffing into him. After one really angry row with his father, he came to my house and flung himself into a chair and shouted 'I'm fed up! I've taken all I can stand!' I told him, 'You don't *have* to take any more! Stand up for yourself!' He went on, 'I want no more of this princing! I want to be an ordinary person. I *must* have a life of my own!'

I said, 'Ah, that's different! You *can't* be an ordinary person. You were born to be King. It's there waiting for you, and you can't escape it.'

Again and again I heard him grumble, 'What does it take to be a good King? You must be a figurehead, a wooden man! Do nothing to upset the Prime Minister or the Court or the Archbishop of Canterbury! Show yourself to the people! Mind your manners! Go to Church! What modern man wants *that* sort of life?'

While it is easy to sympathize whole-heartedly with the Prince, he again failed to appreciate, in his recurring fits of pique, that though *he* considered himself to be a 'modern man', the institution of monarchy itself remained rooted very much in the past. Why, his own father had seen to it that the Court should be as stolid, colourless, and rigidly unprogressive as was that of Queen Victoria during the long mournful years that followed the death of the Prince Consort in 1861. George V may have adored his father, but no trace of Edward VII's life-style would attach itself to his ultra-conservative son. Naturally the sober officers of the Household who surrounded the King were in complete accord with His Majesty's views; and when, on one occasion, the Prince of Wales asked Sir Frederick Ponsonby, Keeper of the Privy Purse, how he thought he was getting on, Ponsonby replied:

Touring the Empire: the
Prince standing on the
observation platform of the
royal train, 1922

'If I may say so, Sir, I think there is risk in your making yourself too accessible.'

When Prince Edward asked him to explain what he meant, Ponsonby went on, 'The monarchy must always retain an element of mystery. A Prince should not show himself too much. The monarchy must remain on a pedestal.'

The young Prince of Wales on the terrace of the House of Commons, with Winston Churchill

Other monarchies had been toppled for much less. But clearly, 'Fritz' Ponsonby spoke not only for himself in imagining that the people respected the monarchy because it hung suspended in a state of semi-mysticism, but for King George V himself.

'If you bring it down to the people,' Sir Frederick said, 'it will lose its mystery and influence.'

The Prince of Wales disagreed, of course, arguing that the times were changing.

Ponsonby's severe reply was tantamount to calling the Heir Apparent an arrogant young puppy. 'I am older than you are, Sir,' he said. 'I have been with your father, your grandfather, and your great-grandmother. They all understood. You are quite mistaken.'

Here once more the old school, frightened of change, suspicious of those who questioned, opposed to those who might probe too deeply, clashed with the new: the servant of a reactionary monarch warning his master's potentially radical successor not to allow daylight to penetrate the shadows of the monarchic machine, lest the illusion should fade for ever.

Could there ever have been a prince more troubled by the position in which something as simple as an accident of birth had placed him? For another prince the 'do as you are told, no questions asked' attitude of the Court might have equalled a near-enviable life, but it was not so for this young Prince. In her memoirs, Mabell, Countess of Airlie, for more than half a century a lady-in-waiting to and an intimate friend of Queen Mary, recalled an unexpected visit from Prince Edward one afternoon, when he explained plaintively that he did not object to doing his job, but did resent the fact that he wasn't allowed what he called a 'free hand'. Lady Airlie wrote:

He sat for over an hour on a stool in front of the fire, smoking one cigarette after another and talking his heart out. He was nervous and frustrated, pulled this way and that. The Queen had told me that she was urging the King to keep him in England . . . to make up for the gap in his constitutional experience caused by the war. [The Prime Minister] Mr Lloyd George on the other hand had evolved a plan for a series of Empire tours.

It was in fact to help preserve the monarchic idyll, as well as to thank the nations of the Empire for the part their armies had played in winning the Great War, that the Prince of Wales was to be dispatched overseas. Before then, however, the Prince moved out of Buckingham Palace, a place he never liked, and with his father's permission established himself at York House, part of the red-brick Palace of St James's, which King Henry VIII had built for his second queen, Anne Boleyn, on the site of a hospital for leprous maidens. Although Prince Edward asked for a house of his own – and who could doubt that it was to escape the King's vigilant eye? – he settled on one with which he was already familiar. York House had been the first official residence in London of George V and Queen Mary, when they were Duke and Duchess of York.

Then, inescapably, came the Empire tours, huge-scale public relations exercises which, particularly this century, have played a very considerable part in the royal way of life. Many young men emerged from the First World War to be hailed as heroes, of course, and the Prince of Wales was no exception. Everywhere his 'Prince Charming' reputation preceded him, and everywhere he was rapturously received.

❊

Travelling aboard HMS *Renown*, Prince Edward set sail from Portsmouth on 5 August 1919, at the start of his first goodwill mission. His destination was the New World: first Canada, then the United States. Landing at St John's in Newfoundland on 12 August, the Prince announced, 'I want Canada to look upon me as a Canadian, if not actually by birth, certainly in mind and spirit.' The peoples of the Dominion took him at his word, and nowhere was he welcomed more enthusiastically than in Quebec where he was literally engulfed by tens of thousands of people, all cheering or yelling words of greeting, all trying to shake his hand or at least to touch him, some even attempting to pull the buttons from his coat. It was a fantastic reception – 'so volatile and vigorous as to constitute at times an almost terrifying phenomenon'. Such scenes were to be repeated again and again. At one parade, some twenty-seven thousand ex-servicemen broke ranks and swarmed around the Prince with such enthusiasm that he had to be lifted from his startled horse and borne over the men's heads to the royal dais. Throughout August, September, and October, the Prince of Wales's schedule took him to Halifax, Charlotte-town, Toronto, Ottawa, Mon-treal, Port Arthur, Fort William, Winnipeg, Saskatoon, Edmonton, Cal-gary, Banff, Vancouver, and the Niagara Falls, with visits to more than thirty towns and cities sandwiched in between.

'What I saw in North America stirred me deeply,' he wrote later, 'most of all the beauty and grandeur of the Canadian Rockies.' So smitten was the Prince that in Alberta he had no hesitation in buying a 4,000-acre ranch in the valley of the Highwood River, forty miles or so from Calgary.

At home Lloyd George, who had maintained that the Dominions wanted 'a first-class carnival in which the Prince of Wales should play a gay, many-sided and natural role', followed the Prince's triumphant progress with intense glee. Having engineered the tours which repeatedly proved the Prince of Wales's sterling abilities as Britain's leading ambassador, the Prime Minister joyfully exclaimed:

The Throne means a great deal in this country. It means even more to the Empire. Throughout all climes, through all continents, there is no institution – Parliament, laws, ecclesiastical organizations, not even language – of which it can be said that it is common to the whole Empire. But the Throne unites them all. You have only to read what happened in Canada to see that the Empire is stronger today for that tour. The welcome was not an organized one; it welled from the hearts of a brave people, and you can see it in every line that comes from Canada and in every word you hear of what happened there. The Prince of Wales struck the right note. He greeted Canada as a nation, as a nation that had won the spurs of nationhood in the great conflict of the nations for freedom and civilization. And that was part of his success.

One almost imagines that such fine rhetoric should have fallen upon an assembly of shining faces, with cacophonous sounds of trumpet flourishes punctuating the Prime Minister's every paragraph. Curiously the efforts of none save royal figures are ever applauded in such fulsome, even florid terms; but even the most cynical observer, cutting right through the premier's euphoric address, would have been hard put to deny the success of the Prince's laborious progress through the Dominion.

From Canada that winter, the Prince of Wales crossed into the United States for a ten-day visit that was certainly no less outstanding. In Washington, where he was treated to a rousing reception, the Prince called upon the ailing President Wilson – who received him at the White House, propped up in Abraham Lincoln's famous monstrosity of a bed, and set the Prince reflecting on the cares of high office, as mirrored in the President's tired and disillusioned face. New York, to quote Lord Kinross, gave Prince Edward 'an ear-splitting harbour welcome, and a "snowstorm" of ticker-tape showered down upon him as he drove up Broadway to be presented to the Mayor with "the freedom of this greatest city of the wonder republic of the ages"'. Viewing the Prince more as a man than as some glittering potentate to be revered, the New York *Sun* said that the future King had won American hearts 'not entirely because he was Prince of Wales', but because of his smile and 'the natural fun-loving spirit that twinkles in his blue eyes'. Exhilarated though the Prince evidently was by this tour, there always lurked beneath the surface a deep melancholy that was rarely, if ever, seen by the bedazzled, fantasy-loving, flag-waving crowds.

One of the Prince of Wales's cousins, as well as a particularly intimate friend, was Lord Mountbatten. He accompanied Prince Edward on his seven-month tour of Australia and New Zealand in 1920, and again on the eight-month-long visit to India, Ceylon, Malaya, Singapore, Hong Kong, and Japan, which began a year later. Mountbatten recalled:

David often got depressed . . . and said he'd like to change places with me. He was moody – had fits of downright gloom. He made a fine appearance, and was attentive to what was required of him, but then one of his fits would come over him – they came like a *flash* – and he'd shut himself in his cabin for days, alone, face drawn, eyes brooding. His staff couldn't go near him. I was the only one who dared intrude, to try to rouse him from his melancholy. He was basically a lonely person, lonely and sad.

Admirably suited to 'princing', yet so tragically miscast as a member of the royal family, Prince Edward's deep-seated melancholia could be attributed to many things. But despite them all, can there really be any doubt that he simply did not want the job royal birth had elected for him?

Royal Ambassador. The Prince flanked by his brothers, the Dukes of Gloucester and York, and Lord Louis Mountbatten (far left)

From the Maoris,
a cloak of Kiwi feathers.
New Zealand, 1920

At any rate, he didn't want it in its existing form. More than a decade later, when, as sovereign, he renounced the uninspiring lot of a royal prince, it was hotly denied that he had never wanted to be king. Even when the Duchess of Windsor came to publish her memoirs during the mid-1950s, she herself made the same emphatic denial. Today, however, whilst making what we will of all the 'alternative' reasons for Prince Edward's behaviour, the evidence constantly leads us back to the argument that the Prince's unhappiness hinged entirely on a role he had never sought and did not want. We shall probably never know for certain whether the twentieth Prince of Wales, for all his anger and depression, ever seriously considered retiring as Heir Apparent. Even if it had been a possibility, the likelihood of his summoning enough courage to put such an idea to the King was extremely remote.

The royal caravan, with its distinguished band of travellers, continued to traverse the Empire. On 26 October 1921, Prince Edward set out for India at the start of the most formidable, yet exotic, tour of his entire career. In 1911, the year of their coronation, King George V and Queen Mary, as Emperor and Empress of India, had made the momentous journey to the subcontinent for the sumptuous coronation durbar in Delhi. Now, a decade later, India's future – if penultimate – Emperor was on his way to visit the brightest jewel in his father's crown.

Sailing once more aboard the *Renown*, the Prince journeyed by way of Gibraltar, Port Said, Suez, and Aden – where he saluted cheering natives mustered beneath a banner which urged him: 'Tell Daddy We Are All Happy Under British Rule' – before arriving in Bombay on 17 November. In contrast to the loyal, and apparently genuine, sentiments expressed in Aden, however, the Prince was to discover that not all Indians were happy with British imperialism. Mahatma Gandhi, the courageous leader of the radical Congress Party and an avowed enemy of the Raj, had just recently launched a campaign of non-co-operation with the Government and had called upon his followers to disrupt the visit of the Prince of Wales.

Fortunately or unfortunately, depending on one's sympathies, the Mahatma's plans were not as successful as he had hoped. In Bombay, whose inhabitants had been enjoined to drape their houses in black, as a sign of mourning at British rule, thousands of Indians turned out to watch the Prince's ceremonial arrival, to hear the speech he delivered on behalf of George V – to which he added, of his own volition, 'I want to know you and I want you to know me' – and to applaud him on his state drive to Government House. Still there were isolated incidents of organized hooliganism, riots, and communal street fighting, all quelled by armed police, but on only one occasion was the Prince's official programme interrupted and then only for the safety of the Indians themselves.

In Lucknow the Mahatma's boycott met with rather more success, when students refused to join in the university sports, shops were closed, and taxi drivers went on strike. This last protest was counteracted by the British Army laying on trucks for those beyond the city perimeters who wanted to see the Prince. Elsewhere in India His Royal Highness received mixed receptions. Yet if the Raj was successful in welcoming the Prince to Delhi, amid what was described as a 'hurricane of cheers', Gandhi's greatest coup occurred in Allahabad. There, in the city of Pandit Nehru – who had been thrown into jail on the eve of the royal party's arrival – the Prince drove through streets of shuttered houses, utterly deserted save for the soldiers who lined the processional route. Even the Prince himself had to agree that it had been 'a spooky experience', and wrote home to his father complaining that he was very depressed about his work in India. 'I don't feel that I'm doing a scrap of good,' he told the King; 'in fact I can say that I know I am not.'

India's future Emperor in Delhi, February 1922

In regions beyond the Mahatma's influence, however, the Prince met the Raj as it survives in the popular imagination today: something between a county garden party at home, polo in Windsor Great Park, and the more genteel scenes from the epic television series *The Jewel in the Crown*. In Jodhpur and Patiala the Prince indulged in the ugly 'sport' of pig-sticking;

in Mysore he played squash with the Maharaja; in Kashmir he rode away on an elephant at the close of a display put on by 'devil dancers'; at Bikaner he inspected the Camel Corps; in Gwalior Edward was greeted by the Maharaja's son and daughter, who had been named George and Mary in honour of the Emperor and Empress; and in Hyderabad parents held their babies aloft 'so that they should grow up with the blessing of having seen the Prince of Wales'.

All very pukkah, and here at least was the stuff of which imperialist memories were made. Fonder memories are, of course, made much nearer home; but one event the Prince of Wales missed entirely while visiting India was the wedding, on 28 February 1922, of the Princess Mary and Viscount Lascelles (later Sixth Earl of Harewood). From London Prince Albert had written to his brother, then to be found somewhere between Agra and Jullundur: 'As far as I can make out, the 28th is going to be a day of national rejoicing.' It was, but how much happier for the only sister he always adored had Prince Edward been in London to celebrate the event with his family.

On 17 March, the Prince of Wales left Karachi and, twenty-six days later, arrived in Yokohama at the start of a month-long visit to Japan as the guest of the present Emperor, then Crown Prince Hirohito. Among the papers still in existence from that time are two particularly entertaining letters written by Sir Charles Eliot, then British Ambassador in Japan, to Lord Curzon, then Secretary of State for Foreign Affairs. Because they provide one or two delightful glimpses of the travelling Prince, it is worth quoting a few paragraphs here.

In one letter Sir Charles says that the Prince 'liked Kyoto', the eighth of his fourteen ports of call in Japan,

where he stopped for a week. There were relatively few functions and he was able to go about informally and enjoy Geisha parties. These latter, I am told on good authority, were strictly platonic, although the Japanese with their usual excess of precaution subjected every female thing that could come near him to a medical examination. In fact it is said that there was nearly a terrible scandal because two missionary ladies who wished to present him with a Japanese Bible were hurried off by the police on the ground that they had not been inspected and disinfected.

Sir Charles then went on to tell Lord Curzon:

Perhaps he sometimes made the mistake of not quite realizing that he was in a foreign country and not in a British possession. He said to me once that though he had travelled

Above Hong Kong, April 1922. The Prince borne in procession by a team of coolies

Below In Japan, 1922. The Prince of Wales (third from left, front row) with 'Dickie' Mountbatten (standing left) and 'Fruity' Metcalfe (standing right)

a great deal he had hardly ever been out of British territory and he seemed to think that he could alter his programme just as he pleased and refuse to go on expeditions for which long and expensive preparations had been made. The senior members of his staff duly reminded him that he was the guest of foreign hosts and then he became penitent for a time. But my most vivid recollection of him is a night interview on the *Renown* at which Admiral Halsey [his comptroller] was present and gave him sound advice as to behaviour in which I endeavoured occasionally to join. H.R.H. was sitting in a large high-backed armchair close to the wall and as the sermon proceeded gradually wriggled upwards until he squatted on the top of the back and from that elevation regarded his two elderly monitors with a most impish and incredulous smile.

Later on towards the end of the Prince's visit to Japan, we find Sir Charles writing to Lord Curzon:

If [the Prince of Wales] seemed a little jaded, he was still able to make use of his remarkable personality when necessary. For instance there was some trouble with the Press. The Japanese Court is very loath to let journalists get near Princes or take photographs and we had to follow their rules, which the newspaper men thought irksome and unnecessary, as the Prince of Wales is himself so democratic. The result was considerable irritation and an indignation meeting, at which it was proposed to boycott H.R.H.'s visit in the Japanese Press and say nothing about it. The next day the Prince received a few of the principal newspaper men and by a brief speech entirely won their hearts, so much so that the man who had been foremost in proposing the boycott entirely recanted and promised to do his best to secure favourable notices . . . . It was also very noticeable how his presence animated the Japanese Court: even the Empress became slightly skittish.

H.R.H. did not seem to have a high opinion of British officials in the East. He told me that the governors of Hong Kong and Singapore were fossilized clerks who ought to be kept in a cupboard in Whitehall. Lord Reading, he said, was 'merely clever' but not at all the right man for Viceroy [of India]. . . . Unfortunately this conversation took place when many Japanese were close by and H.R.H. spoke so loud that I had to remind him that our neighbours understood English.

Many years later, in March 1970, when the distinguished author Kenneth Rose wrote to the Duke of Windsor, reminding him of these amusing incidents, His Royal Highness replied:

The Duchess loved the paragraph about the Geisha girls and the two missionaries. Those parties were indeed strictly platonic so far as I was concerned. I am glad that I have since learned to be more considerate of the organizers of official programs. I also liked my appraisal of the British colonial functionaries, and even Lord Reading in India in those days, which I am afraid were all too true.

In his role as roving ambassador, the Prince of Wales continued his tours of duty until about 1934, when the pursuit of pleasure became a more prominent feature in his life. But all might have changed rather sooner than that, for in November 1928 King George V was taken seriously ill with what was diagnosed as a streptococcal infection of the chest. By the beginning of December, the King's condition was sufficiently alarming for the heir to the throne to be recalled to London. At that time, having completed an official visit to Egypt, Prince Edward was in Africa on safari with Baron Bror von Blixen-Finecke, his wife Karen – better known as the writer Isak Dinesen, author of *Out of Africa* – and Karen's lover Denys Finch Hatton, son of the Earl of Winchelsea.

When news of his father's illness reached him at Dodoma, the Prince remarked, in retrospect rather callously, 'To think that in a few days I may be King of England.'

'And what, Sir, will you do then?' asked one of his companions.

In cavalier mood, the Prince replied, 'I shall do exactly what I like!'

– 4 –

THE FORT AND
MRS SIMPSON

DOING EXACTLY WHAT HE LIKED was all part of Prince Edward's impossible dream. Yet, even as he prepared for his African tour in the summer of 1928, it may be said that destiny unveiled the second phase of the plan it had hatched in Belgrave Square more than ten years earlier. For there had recently arrived in London from the United States the one woman who would fuel some of the Prince's most fantastic notions.

Wallis Warfield Spencer was a thirty-two-year-old divorcee when Maud Kerr-Smiley's brother Ernest Simpson – a former second lieutenant in the Grenadier Guards and now working for the family shipping business – took her as his second wife at Chelsea Register Office on 21 July 1928. Although his father was English and his mother American, Ernest was in some ways more British than the British. He had first met Wallis through mutual friends, Mary and Jacques Raffray, in 1927. Before long the Simpsons had set up home at No. 5 Bryanston Court, not far from Hyde Park Corner. Yet while they were financially well off, they knew hardly anybody. The social linchpin in their lives was Mrs Kerr-Smiley who, at least to begin with, was happy to take Wallis and Ernest beneath her wing. Finding her feet in London society, the new Mrs Simpson soon began to establish a circle of friends of her own, including fellow Americans Benjamin and Consuelo Thaw. The eminently placed Mrs Thaw subsequently introduced Wallis to her sister Thelma, Viscountess Furness, and in turn Lady Furness introduced Mrs Simpson to the Prince of Wales.

In the Britain of the 1920s and 1930s (and in some circles it remains almost as true today) society was more concerned with the pedigree of a new 'recruit' than with his or her own personal attributes. Thus one of the questions that sprung to the lips of the class-conscious was, 'Who *is* Mrs Simpson?'

Wallis Simpson wearing a
blouse embroidered with
her initials, 1935

At the time of the Abdication, when Wallis Simpson became a household name, the entire nation – if not the entire Western hemisphere – was asking the same question. But by then quite *who* she was was a matter of much greater importance. Rumour had it, for example, that Wallis Simpson was a woman of low birth and no breeding who, at least in her second marriage, had struck it comparatively rich. 'You'd think that we'd all come right out of *Tobacco Road!*' Mrs D. Buchanan Merryman, Wallis's beloved 'Aunt Bessie' and closest living relation declared angrily.

Being part of a 'good family' in the freer and more democratic United States, however, was by no means the same as being part of a 'good' family in feudal Great Britain. To be considered entirely acceptable, a person had to belong to a family whose line comfortably spanned several centuries, whose fortune was based very largely on inherited wealth – or 'old money', as it is still called today – and whose social standing was reflected in, among other things, ownership of sufficient acreage in one of the shires.

In America's social strata, although she couldn't boast direct or indirect descent from kings, princes, dukes, or earls, Wallis Simpson's antecedents were impeccable. Here was no ordinary Southern belle, but the daughter of two of America's oldest families: the Warfields of Maryland and the Montagues of Virginia. In an article first published in *The Times Literary Supplement* of 1 November 1974 (and later referred to in *The Windsor Story*, by Messrs Bryan and Murphy, from which I quote) the British journalist Alastair Forbes wrote of the Duchess of Windsor: 'She can be said to come from a far higher stratum than, say, Princess Grace of Monaco, Jacqueline Bouvier (Kennedy Onassis) or the Jerome or Vanderbilt ladies of the nineteenth century. By present English standards of birth, she might rank rather below two recent royal duchesses, and rather above two others.'

Born in a summer holiday cottage at Blue Ridge Summit in Pennsylvania on 19 June 1896, Bessie Wallis – the unflattering names paid tribute to her aunt and her father – was the only child of Teackle Wallis Warfield and his wife Alice (sometimes 'Alys') Montague. The Warfields, who settled in America in 1662, became established as a proud, puritanical, but above all highly successful family; its members were noted bankers, business men, and public servants. One of Wallis's forebears, Edwin Warfield, became Governor of Maryland. The Montagues, although no less politically active, were a more colourful and light-hearted family, whose line spoke of judges and generals and, in time, a Governor of Virginia, too.

Edward of Wales

His Royal Highness Prince Edward in cadet uniform,
aged fourteen. A chalk portrait by W. Strang, signed by the Prince, 1909

Wallis Simpson at forty: a portrait

Prince Edward in his garter robes in 1912,
one year after he was created Prince of Wales

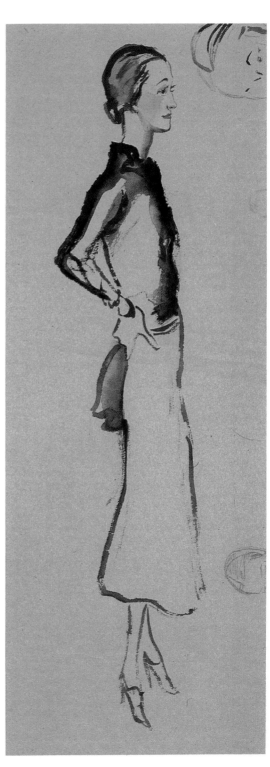

Edward VIII became the first English king to fly. In this study he is seen passing over Windsor Castle

The coat-of-arms of HRH The Duke of Windsor

Right The Duke and Duchess of Windsor, photographed by Karsh of Ottawa. This is one of the last photographs of the Duke

At the age of seventy-five, the
Duchess of Windsor had lost
none of the elegance for which
she was justly famous.
*Photograph by Karsh of
Ottawa*

The Duke and Duchess in the
garden of the Mill, le Moulin de
la Tuilerie, their country house
near Paris, in the late 1960s

The Duke of Windsor's coffin
arriving at RAF Benson in
Oxfordshire

The lying-in-state of the Duke of Windsor, June 1972. In the nave of St George's Chapel, the Duke's coffin, draped with his personal standard and attended by officers of the Grenadier Guards, lay near the tombs of his parents, King George V and Queen Mary, and his successor, King George VI

Yet while her father – who had always suffered from ill-health, but who seems never to have made provision for his family, despite that fact – died when she was only five months old, Wallis had a happy childhood. Plunged into what might reasonably be called a state of genteel poverty, the plight of Alice Montague Warfield was relieved somewhat by the benificence of her dead husband's brother, Solomon. It was 'Uncle Sol', president of the Continental Trust Company, who paid for his niece's education at a fashionable day school in Baltimore and who covered his sister-in-law's bills until she remarried in 1908. Thereafter Wallis became the responsibility of her stepfather, J. F. Raisin, son of the Democratic Party leader; but when he died, early in 1913, mother and daughter again sought the generosity of Solomon Warfield. Not long afterwards Wallis, who was then eighteen, left Oldfields, a highly fashionable boarding-school to which she had been admitted at the age of sixteen, and, on Christmas Eve 1914, made her social début in Baltimore, at a ball known as the Bachelors' Cotillion.

Some months later, Wallis received an invitation from a cousin, Mrs Corinne Mustin, to visit her at the recently established Pensacola Air Station in Florida, where her husband was commandant. Flying was at that time still daringly new, and, perhaps not surprisingly, the airmen themselves were looked upon as a daringly new breed of hero. Never was this truer than when they became embroiled in the Great War, then raging in distant Europe. Within a day of her arrival at Pensacola, Wallis met and became fatally attracted to Lieutenant Earl Winfield Spencer, of the United States Navy. In *The Heart Has Its Reasons* she recalled writing home to her mother: 'I have just met the world's most fascinating aviator.'

Alice Montague Warfield expressed no surprise but, like most mothers of young daughters, sounded a word of caution. The life of a Navy wife, she said, 'would be hard enough at best – no permanent home, a constant change of station, little money, and long and lonely waits for a husband to return from the sea'. Then, although she could not have realized that her advice would be equally suited to Wallis's future royal marriage, had it occurred in more agreeable circumstances, Mrs Warfield added: 'The Navy, too, requires conformity to its own code. I fear you may well be too spirited, too independent to take easily to so regulated a life.'

Happy and in love, Wallis dismissed her mother's concern as 'unreal and irrelevant'. About a year later, during the early evening of 8 November 1916, dressed in white panne velvet, embroidered with pearls, a circlet of orange-blossom crowning a long white tulle veil, Wallis walked up the aisle at Christ Church, Baltimore, on the arm of 'Uncle Sol', who gave her in marriage to 'Win' Spencer. Among the seven young women who attended the bride that night was Wallis's old school-friend Mary Kirk, who, in yet another twist to this very strange story, was eventually to succeed Wallis herself, as the third wife of Ernest Simpson.

✳

Whatever dreams the new Mrs Earl Winfield Spencer may have had about life with her 'fascinating aviator', reality soon put paid to them in brutal fashion. The man she had married, itching for combat duty in the skies over Europe, was dispatched instead to Squantum, Massachusetts, near Boston, to take command of the new naval air station there. So great was his success that he was subsequently detailed to organize the naval air station on North Island, California.

The future Duchess of Windsor in 1915 at the age of nineteen

With the Armistice in 1918, however, Win Spencer, already dispirited and disenchanted, became angry and embittered. Making enemies where he needed allies, he started to drink heavily; his moods grew darker and increasingly difficult to handle. In her memoirs, the Duchess of Windsor recalled: 'since nothing was right in the office, nothing was right at home. Whatever I did was wrong in Win's eyes, and in this unhappy situation, he did what was so easy for him – he took to the bottle.' Living in a thin-walled service apartment with a man who 'was not a quiet drinker' meant that, in Wallis's words, 'I had the humiliation of having our private difficulties become known to our friends. I pleaded with my husband to save such remnants of dignity and self-respect as were still left to us.' Instead Wallis, who on one occasion had been thrown into the bathroom and kept locked up for the best part of a day, watched aghast at the transformation of her husband's character. From 'a brilliant officer' he became 'a mixed-up neurotic'.

To the horror of her mother and her Aunt Bessie, Wallis contemplated divorce, reasoning that since she always took the brunt of Win's fury, his life might be made easier if she were no longer a part of it. Alice Montague Raisin's utter dismay at her daughter's news was echoed by Aunt Bessie's formidable declaration that 'Montague women do not get divorced.' For the Warfields Uncle Sol exploded, 'I won't let you bring this disgrace upon us!' In the event, any immediate divorce action was delayed by separation. Wallis went to stay with her mother in Washington and almost immediately found herself caught up in the social whirl of parties and receptions.

Having 'a good time' was an expression that frequently passed Wallis's lips, and in the capital, Don Felipe Espil, first secretary at the Argentinian Embassy, ensured that she was not disappointed. Yet there were also the not-so-good times when she felt lonely, and when Win Spencer – who had continued to write to her – begged Wallis to join him in China, where he had been posted in 1922, she agreed to go. At government expense, therefore, she boarded the USS *Chaumont* on 17 July 1924 and sailed to the Philippines. There she changed ships and aboard the *Empress of Canada* completed the voyage to Hong Kong where Win waited to greet her. For a little while all was well between the Spencers, but when his drinking started again, accompanied by all the familiar moods and petty jealousies, Wallis faced the fact that the marriage was at an end. In December 1927, she and Earl Winfield Spencer were finally divorced.

Interestingly enough it was at about this time that a fortune-teller in

New York told the future Duchess that she would have two more husbands and become 'a famous woman'. Not long before, Wallis had tried her hand at selling tubular steel in order to finance herself, but while that job hadn't worked out, she wondered if the predicted 'fame' was still connected in some way with a business venture. (In a rare television interview, given more than thirty years later, the Duchess of Windsor told Kenneth Harris of the BBC that she would have liked to head an advertising agency.)

The fortune-teller firmly ruled out a life in the world of commerce, however, and informed Wallis: 'There is nothing in your aura to suggest an association with a business career. You will lead a woman's life, marrying, divorcing, marrying again, with several emotional crises. The power that is to come to you will be related to a man.'

That prophecy, as Wallis was soon to discover, began to prove itself not long after she and Ernest Simpson established themselves in London.

Ernest Simpson, whom Wallis Spencer married in July 1928

For Edward, Prince of Wales, the start of the 1930s – perhaps the most important and certainly the most decisive, decade of his entire life – afforded another opportunity to distance himself from the Court of King George V, albeit on a purely personal level. Already possessed of an official residence at York House, St James's Palace, the King now permitted him to acquire a private retreat on the very edge of Windsor Great Park, at Sunningdale in Berkshire.

To the Prince, who came to adore it, Fort Belvedere was a 'castellated conglomeration', 'a pseudo-Gothic hodge podge'. To the King, it was 'a queer old place'. To most of the Prince of Wales's regular week-end guests it was, in the words of Lady Diana Cooper, 'a child's idea of a fort' – a castle in miniature that only needed 'fifty red soldiers stood between the battlements to make it into a Walt Disney coloured symphony toy'. All these descriptions still apply today, fifty years after the Duke of Windsor drove out of the Fort's wooden gates for the last time. Indeed, even though it seems strangely ill-suited to non-royal ownership, Fort Belvedere – as the present author discovered – truly remains the 'enchanting folly' that the Prince's friends knew so well half a century ago.

Swinging abruptly off the A329 Ascot–Bracknell road, not far from the ruins of George IV's 'Fishing Temple' at Virginia Water, where King Edward VII celebrated the birth of his first grandson during an Ascot-week ball, the estate is to be found concealed from public view by thickly wooded grounds. Beyond, the mellow-stone Fort itself stands majestically at the top of a hill, the house surmounted by a solitary tower from which, both as Prince of Wales and briefly as King, the Duke of Windsor always flew the Duke of Cornwall's standard. As Heir Apparent Prince Edward, like Prince Charles today, was also the Duke of Cornwall; and that largely unfamiliar banner was intended to inform visitors that this was not a formal place of royal residence, but a private bolt-hole, a 'resting-place' for a 'rolling stone', as Prince Edward himself once put it.

Beneath the drawing-room windows, looking out towards Virginia Water, lie the semi-circular battlements, on which are stationed twenty-three eighteenth-century bronze cannons, now green with age. Below the terrace, and completely unspoilt by successive owners, is the famous swimming-pool, once nothing more than 'a muddy lily pond', upon which so much of the Fort's social life was centred in summer. On the far side of the broad arc formed by the battlements lies the tennis court and a little further still is the sloping glade that until recently had always been known

Fort Belvedere, Sunningdale, seen from the battlements

The octagonal drawing-room at Fort Belvedere, where Edward VIII signed the Instrument of Abdication

A great tea-drinker; the
Prince relaxing by the
swimming-pool at the Fort

as the Cedar Walk, its name taken from the vast trees that grow there.
Somewhat fancifully, it has now been rechristened the Duchess's Walk.

Today, if the spirit of the Duke of Windsor exists anywhere at Fort
Belvedere, it is most assuredly in the garden that he lovingly created (the
herbaceous border skirting the battlements remains exactly as he laid it
out) and in the grounds beyond, where he and his guests – sometimes
reluctant helpers – struggled to clear the tangled undergrowth, that had no
doubt flourished unchecked ever since the 1820s when George IV commissioned Wyatville to enlarge the original 'gazebo', built for the Duke of
Cumberland.

The house, or rather the Fort itself, also remains unaltered – at least
structurally. From the double front doors a bright hallway veers off to an
octagonal lobby. Here the Prince and his guests often danced to the
gramophone on the black-and-white marble floor, and here, in his day,
chairs upholstered in yellow leather stood in each of the eight corners. Two
rooms led directly off this inner hall: the Library, which the Prince of Wales

used as a bedroom complete with *en suite* bathroom; and the magnificent octagonal drawing-room, panelled in soft, natural pine. In this wide and spacious room, with its Chippendale furniture, Canalettos from the Royal Collection were hung on the panelled walls, and yellow velvet curtains dressed the tall Gothic windows. Despite its splendid paintings, furnishings, and *objets d'art*, Fort Belvedere remained a warm, relaxed, and unpretentious house where, as Lady Diana Cooper recalled in her memoirs, the comfort could not have been greater, 'nor the desire on [the Prince's] part for his guests to be happy, free and unembarrassed'.

Left Beside the pool with Linda, daughter of Major 'Fruity' Metcalfe and his wife, Lady Alexandra

Right The Prince with his equerry, 'Fruity' Metcalfe, and 'Dickie' Mountbatten at Fort Belvedere

✳

Wallis Simpson, then the wife of Lieutenant Earl Winfield Spencer, had first met the Prince of Wales in San Diego in April 1920, during a reception given in His Royal Highness's honour by Vice-Admiral Clarence Williams, on board his flagship, the USS *New Mexico*. That meeting, however, doubtless no more than a brief exchange of pleasantries, is invariably overlooked in favour of one which the Duchess of Windsor always maintained took place at a house party given by Thelma, Lady Furness, at Melton Mowbray, Leicestershire, in November 1930, but which, according to the Duke, did not take place until twelve months later, during the winter of 1931.

Whenever their second meeting occurred, and the date is of little real significance, the story of the Prince and Mrs Simpson was not to begin until 1932 when, 'out of the blue', Prince Edward invited Wallis and her husband to be his guests at Fort Belvedere, for the weekend of 30 January. Thelma Furness would, as usual, act as the Prince's hostess, and Wallis's fellow guests were to include her friends the Thaws. As Duchess of Windsor, Mrs Simpson was to recall:

Ernest and I drove out in the late afternoon, timing our pace to arrive at six. It was dark when we approached the Fort. Our headlights picked out a gravel driveway winding in graceful turns through a wood; suddenly there materialized a fascinating, shadowy mass, irregular in outline and of different levels . . . bathed in soft light thrown up by concealed flood-lamps. Even before the car ground to a stop, the door opened and a servant appeared. An instant later the Prince himself was at the door to welcome his guests and supervise the unloading of our luggage. . . .

The Prince himself insisted on taking us to our room . . . and I could not help noticing that before he left he swiftly appraised the condition of the room with the practised glance of a careful host, a side of his character that was totally unexpected. Having assured himself that all was as it should be, he left us, saying he would expect us down shortly for cocktails.

If the Prince's courtesy in showing his new friends to their room had surprised the Simpsons, Wallis was even more surprised on entering the drawing-room to find her host doing needlepoint. Rising from the sofa, the Prince laughingly told her that this was his 'secret vice' and added, 'the only one I am at pains to conceal'. Then, with what Wallis described as part amusement and part pride, he showed her the covering intended for a backgammon table that he was working on. Had she but known it then, the chair that she sat on in the dining-room that night was also covered in the Prince's handiwork, as were the remaining nine chairs positioned round the walnut dining-table.

The art of *gros point*, as Prince Edward explained, had been taught to him – and to his brothers, for that matter – by Queen Mary, who was justly famous for the works she created, including an enormous carpet that went on public display when completed. The discovery of the Prince's pastime touched Wallis and, once again in her own words: 'I decided then and there that he must have a really sweet and tender side to his nature.'

He did have such a side, of course, but there was also in his make-up a shocking thoughtlessness that made some of his actions indefensible. While warming to Mrs Simpson's transatlantic charms – and in June 1933 he honoured her with a party at Quaglino's to celebrate her thirty-seventh birthday – Prince Edward began to tire of both Lady Furness and Mrs Dudley Ward, who between them had devoted twenty-one years to his personal service. Both were dismissed early in 1934 and both in similar fashion.

Thelma, Viscountess Furness (second from right) with her sister Gloria Vanderbilt and friends

The first to go was Thelma Furness who, upon returning from a visit to the United States, complained to Wallis – to whom the Prince had been 'entrusted' during her absence – that their royal friend seemed to be avoiding her. Invitations to the Fort had ceased to arrive, and, even more coldly, whenever she telephoned, her calls were refused. Presently the curtain also fell on the Prince's long-standing relationship with Freda Dudley Ward. Lady Donaldson tells us:

In May 1934 Mrs Dudley Ward's elder daughter had an operation for appendicitis, followed unexpectedly by complications. For several weeks she was seriously ill. During these weeks her mother thought of little else and spent most of her time at the nursing home. Only when her daughter was out of danger and on the way to recovery did she begin to consider the fact that, for the first time in nearly seventeen years . . . a period of weeks had gone by without [the Prince of Wales] visiting her house or telephoning her.

It was then that Mrs Dudley Ward called York House, only to hear the distressed switchboard operator say, 'I have something so terrible to tell you, that I don't know how to say it – I have orders not to put you through.' Neither Lady Furness nor Mrs Dudley Ward ever heard from the Prince again.

KING EDWARD VIII

ALTHOUGH SHE COULD HARDLY have realized it at the time, Wallis Simpson's star had begun its climb towards ignominy while Thelma Furness was away in New York at the start of 1934. At the age of forty, the Prince of Wales had finally found his 'perfect woman'. As his feelings towards her grew daily more obsessive, and word spread rapidly along society's grapevine, so an ever increasing number of people clamoured to meet the new royal favourite – or, at least, were sufficiently curious to do so, when the opportunity arose. Among those enthralled by events in the Prince's life was Chips Channon, an ambitious social-mountaineering American, who came from Chicago in 1918, avidly collected celebrities, among them Lady Honor Guinness, whom he married, became a Member of Parliament, and was eventually knighted. His diaries, more a social history of the times, span three decades and provide a detailed insight into the fashionable world that adopted him.

On 14 May 1935, Channon wrote:

There is tremendous excitement about Mrs Simpson who has now banned ——* and all her group from York House. It is war to the knife between the past and the present. Mrs Simpson has enormously improved the Prince. In fact, the romance surpasses all else in interest. He is obviously madly infatuated and she, a jolly unprepossessing American, witty, a mimic, an excellent cook, has completely subjugated him. Never has he been so in love. She is madly anxious to storm society, while she still is his favourite, so that when he leaves her (as he leaves everyone in time) she will be secure.

To the distinguished diplomat Harold Nicolson, who was married to the poet and novelist Vita Sackville-West, Wallis Simpson was 'a perfectly harmless type of American'. However, very much later he was to tell James Pope-Hennessy, Queen Mary's official biographer, that 'Rich vulgarity like that of Mrs Simpson is worse than poor vulgarity.'

* Name deleted – but would that of Thelma Furness be too obvious a guess?

To Cecil Beaton, friend and photographer of royalty, designer, artist, writer and international celebrity, Wallis was at first 'a brawny great cow or bullock in sapphic blue velvet. . . . To hear her speak was enough,' Beaton wrote. 'Her voice was raucous and appalling. I thought her awful, common, vulgar, strident, a second-rate American with no charm.' Later on his opinion changed radically, and she became bright, witty and chic, in short, 'all that is elegant. . . . I am certain she has more glamour and is of more interest than any public figure.' In Lady Diana Cooper's opinion Mrs Simpson 'was hard through and through, but exhilarating. The room came alive when she came in.' Henceforth society would ever remain divided in its opinions of the Prince's 'moll', as one American newspaper described her; divided, yet nevertheless fascinated.

From girlhood, Wallis had always been deeply attractive to the opposite sex, trailing in her wake a number of admirers, boyfriends and lovers. Yet while she was fully experienced in the ways of the world, her 'glamour' was not of an overtly physical or sexual kind. Instead it emanated from the sheer force and energy of her personality. At about the time she fell from grace, Lady Furness wrote of Mrs Simpson:

She did not have the chic she has since cultivated. She was not beautiful; in fact she was not even pretty. But she had a distinct charm and a sharp sense of humour. Her dark hair was parted in the middle [a style she had adopted in her teens, and would retain all her life]. Her eyes, alert and eloquent, were her best feature. She was not as thin as in her later years – not that she could be called fat even then; she was merely less angular. Her hands were large; they did not move gracefully, and I thought she used them too much when she attempted to emphasise a point.

Regardless of who did or did not like Wallis Simpson, however – and the subsequent image of her as a brash, fast-living Jezebel is an unjust one – there were more than enough people in and around the Prince of Wales's circle, the likes of Chips Channon, Emerald Cunard, and Sybil Colefax, who were only too ready to 'suck up' to her and, in the Prince's hearing, give loud assurance that it was 'marvellous' to have her around. Of course, when the crunch came and the Abdication burst that particular royal bubble, there was to be heard a frantic scuttling of feet as the couple's 'friends' rushed to nail their colours very firmly to the new King's mast.

❋

The Prince of Wales had first dined with the Simpsons at Bryanston Court

A highland holiday: the Princesses Elizabeth and Margaret with their Uncle David

in July 1933. He had asked if he might look in one evening and had stayed well beyond the cocktail hour. Wallis's invitation to remain for dinner with Ernest and herself, provided he didn't mind taking pot luck, was happily accepted. Thereafter, the Prince started to become a regular caller, popping in unexpectedly on weekday evenings and accepting invitations to the Simpsons' cocktail and dinner parties without a moment's hesitation. After a while Simpson began to excuse himself, saying that he had business paperwork to catch up with, although in time, despite his love of everything royal, he grew resentful of the Heir Apparent's repeated and, as he saw it, intrusive appearances. This in turn caused such friction between Mr and Mrs Simpson that Wallis was in due course forced to admonish the Prince for his selfish and unfair behaviour.

For the Simpsons themselves, this was the beginning of the end. Slowly, almost imperceptibly – or so it would seem – Ernest started to become as much of a shadowy presence in Wallis's life as he became a prominent feature in that of her old friend Mary Raffray who was eventually to become the third Mrs Ernest Simpson.

It must be said, however, that until the beginning of 1934 Wallis had genuinely believed the Prince of Wales's infatuation with her to be no more than a passing phase; something to be looked back upon in later years, with amusement and affection. That her 'reign' would one day end, just as surely as those of her two predecessors had ended, seemed to Mrs Simpson a foregone conclusion. Then, as summer approached, the Prince invited the Simpsons to make up his holiday party in Biarritz that August. Ernest again cried off, this time because of a business trip to the United States; but Wallis – who asked her Aunt Bessie Merryman to act as chaperon – had no reservations about accepting, even though she was already living on borrowed money in order to keep up with the jazzy, immensely rich circle surrounding the man she called her 'blue-eyed charmer'.

During that holiday, the Prince and his guests took a cruise aboard Lord Moyne's yacht, the *Rosaura*, and it was then, in the Duchess of Windsor's own words, that she and the Prince of Wales 'crossed the line that marks the indefinable boundary between friendship and love'. As we have already seen, Wallis Simpson, stylish, vivacious, and shrewd, a woman with great flair, was clearly a considerable personality in her own right. Yet all the same, she was most decidedly *not* the kind of woman British princes normally married. What then was the attraction?

Siren-esque Mrs Simpson undoubtedly was – in her own way. But while

Above George V out riding with his sons 'David', 'Bertie', 'Harry' and 'George'

Below King George V, with Queen Mary, addressing Parliament on the occasion of his Silver Jubilee in May 1935. Their sons listen: left to right, the Duke of Gloucester, the Prince of Wales, the Duke of York and the Duke of Kent

she could certainly have been described as a dangerously fascinating woman, she was no voluptuous seductress, bent on luring her Prince Charming towards disaster. In fact, while blame for the Abdication has always been laid squarely on Wallis's shoulders, it has to be admitted that the Prince of Wales captained his own ship, as indeed he had always intended to do, and it was by *his* hand, not Mrs Simpson's, that it came to grief. 'Establishmentarians' have always adopted a quite different attitude, preferring to use the American divorcee as a scapegoat, rather than acknowledge the simple truth that Edward, Prince of Wales, for all his winning ways, was essentially weak; a man who yearned to be dominated; a man who searched for the kind of love his own mother was unable to give, and who eventually found what he was looking for in a relationship that was distinctly redolent of the 'master/slave' syndrome.

Looking back to his childhood, it is perfectly possible to accept the argument that the Prince of Wales – the son of an intimidating father, raised by nannies, governed by tutors, and subjected to the strict regimes of two naval colleges – could never escape the need for an authoritarian presence towering over him. But did his emotional needs run even deeper than that? We may never know for sure; but it might well be true, as has occasionally been suggested, that the Prince of Wales fought to suppress an innate tendency towards homosexuality.

In a colourful contemporary vignette, Lytton Strachey told a curious tale of having seen the Prince during a visit to the National Gallery in London. On 10 June 1930, Strachey reported to Dora Carrington:

I went yesterday to see the Duveen room – a decidedly twilight effect: but spacing out the Italian pictures produces on the whole a fair effect. There was a black-haired tart marching round in india-rubber boots, and longing to be picked up. We both lingered in the strangest manner in front of various masterpieces – wandering from room to room. Then on looking round I perceived a more attractive tart – fair-haired this time – bright yellow and thick hair – a pink face – and plenty of vitality. So I transferred my attentions, and began to move in his direction when on looking more closely I observed that it was the Prince of Wales – no doubt at all – a Custodian bowing and scraping, and Philip Sassoon also in attendance. I then became terrified that the latter would see me, and insist on performing an introduction, so I fled – perhaps foolishly – perhaps it might have been the beginning of a really entertaining affair.

The implications behind Strachey's story, although circumstantial, are sufficiently clear. But whether he was indulging in wishful thinking, or

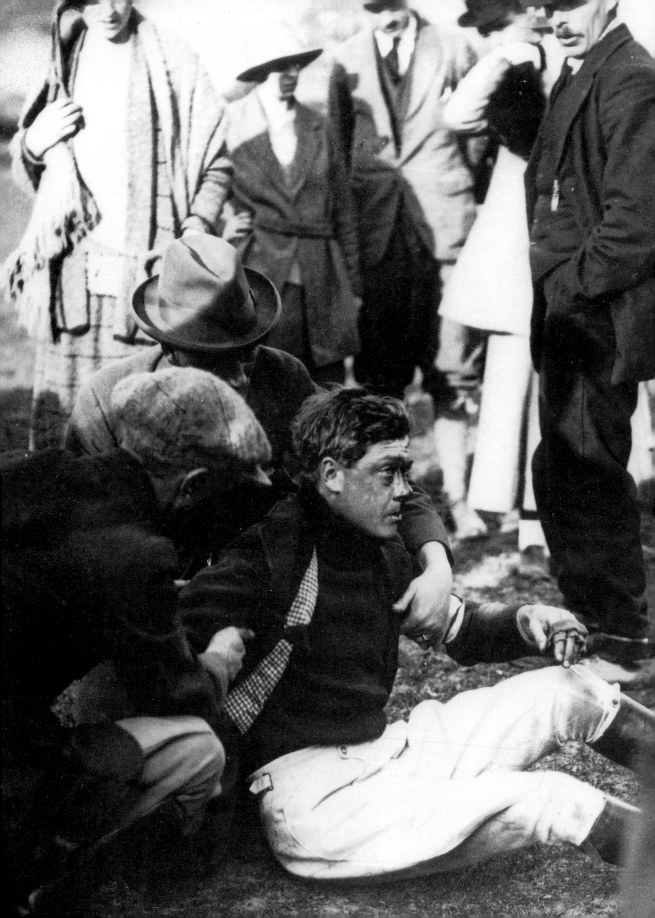

revealing a modicum of 'inside' knowledge, is up to the individual to decide. On the other hand, a number of psychologists have reasoned that many men – fearful that the potential may lie within themselves – not only react with hostility towards the whole concept of homosexuality, but may seek to exert their own masculinity through the pursuit of physically demanding activities, frequently in sport. Without contriving to make the facts fit the argument, it is interesting to remember that, after a shaky start, the Prince of Wales became a competent rider, an enthusiastic though sometimes foolhardy fox-hunter, and a steeplechaser whose recklessness landed him in a darkened room for a week, recovering from concussion, and kept him in bed for a month thereafter. 'Hunting and steeple-chasing were more than exhilarating exercise to me,' the Prince wrote; 'they satisfied the latent desire in me to excel; to pit myself against others on equal terms; to show that, at least in matters where physical boldness and endurance counted, I could hold my own.'

The Prince's need to prove himself in competitive sport may conceivably tell us something, but a remark made by one of his oldest friends is yet more revealing. The Prince of Wales, the author was told, '*despised* homosexuals and would never have them in the house'. Such a statement is as absurd as it is patently untrue. For while members of the royal family may be expected to strike an *official* attitude of disapproval towards something that challenges society's view of 'normality', in private it has always been a very different matter. Indeed, royal figures have invariably gathered about them, among their friends, their courtiers, and their servants – to say nothing of their own relations – a great many of homosexual persuasion. Moreover, during the early 1950s one of the Duchess of Windsor's closest friends was an American well known for his sexual preferences. He was Jimmy Donahue, rich, flamboyant, the grand-son of Frank W. Woolworth, and for three or four years a conspicuous member of the Windsor coterie. Here, then, was at least one undisguised homosexual who was not only a welcome guest of the Duke and Duchess, but who was on terms of considerable intimacy with them both.

Taken in isolation none of these things may appear to mean a great deal. Together they form the basis of a plausible theory, one that is made a little more intriguing by the assertion that there was in Wallis Simpson herself an element of masculinity. In her biography of Edward VIII, for example, Frances Donaldson tells us that, some time during the 1930s, a member of Prime Minister Stanley Baldwin's entourage 'amused himself by sending a

The Prince after a bad fall at
a point-to-point near
Wokingham, Surrey

specimen of Mrs Simpson's handwriting to a graphologist'. The analysis revealed 'a woman with a strong male inclination in the sense of activity, vitality, initiative. She *must* dominate, she *must* have authority'.

Mrs Simpson's 'masculine' streak may, for all we know, have struck a very particular chord in the Prince of Wales's psyche. And if that were mirrored in some dark way in his search for one powerful enough to fulfil the dual role of, say, surrogate mother *and* lover, then it requires little imagination to understand why Wallis Simpson – as no other woman – occupied a position of unparalleled importance in the Prince's life.

We may also find a further clue to the depth of the Prince of Wales's confused sexual identity in a remarkably outspoken interview which the Duchess of Windsor gave towards the end of her life, to the writer Dennis Eisenberg. Of her husband, the Duchess said,

He had a terrible problem, you see. He had been brought up by very strict parents . . . harsh and authoritarian. The atmosphere at Buckingham Palace was incredibly Victorian, prudish and narrow-minded.

To make it worse, David had a deeply sensitive soul. After reaching adulthood he quarrelled bitterly with his father over everything. After getting to know David and realizing that he was a desperately shy young man, full of deeply ingrained inhibitions of the most incredible kind, it became clear that he could not have been a wild libertine.

In those days, people never spoke about such things. But I had been married twice and knew instinctively that he had never really fulfilled himself in a mature, adult relationship with a member of the opposite sex. I loved David for his wonderful spirit and his fine mind. In time, when he grew to know and trust me, our relationship became a totally fulfilled one.

I realized eventually that he was truly happy with an understanding woman for the first and only time in his life.

✳

Mrs Simpson was presented to the Prince's parents, King George V and Queen Mary, on only two occasions, the first at a Court given at Buckingham Palace in June 1931, the second at a reception in November 1934, held to celebrate the marriage of Prince George, Duke of Kent, and Princess Marina of Greece and Denmark. On that occasion the Prince of Wales approached his mother with the words, 'I want to introduce a great friend of mine.' The Queen politely shook hands with Wallis and no doubt exchanged a perfunctory greeting. Two years later, however, she remarked

King George V at the time of his Silver Jubilee, 1935

Majestic but aloof: a study of Queen Mary, signed 1936

Ski-ing with his favourite brother, Prince George, Duke of Kent

ruefully to her old friend Mabell, Lady Airlie, 'If I had only guessed then I might perhaps have been able to do something, but now it's too late.'

Quite what Queen Mary thought she might have been able to do in order to save the Prince of Wales from himself is hard to imagine; but by the time she opened her eyes to what was happening, her son was past redemption. Given that Mrs Simpson undoubtedly made no greater impression on Queen Mary than any other member of the Prince of Wales's set, it is hardly surprising that she failed to realize the extent of the Prince's preoccupation. We must also bear in mind that throughout 1935 the Queen was engrossed not only in her own official calendar of engagements but in the celebrations marking the Silver Jubilee of her husband's reign. Also taking place in that year, albeit on a much smaller scale, was the wedding, in November, of her third son, Prince Henry, Duke of Gloucester and Lady Alice Montagu-Douglas-Scott, daughter of the Seventh Duke of Buccleuch. Then, almost immediately came the final dramatic decline in George V's health, precipitated by the recurrence of bronchial trouble that had first started to plague him several years earlier.

At Sandringham on Friday 17 January 1936, the King made his last, virtually illegible entry in the diary he had faithfully kept for almost sixty years. Commenting on the snow and wind, he wrote: 'Dawson [Lord Dawson of Penn, the royal physician] arrived this evening. I saw him and feel rotten.' Three days later, only five minutes before midnight on 20 January, the seventy-year-old monarch died. At that moment, Edward, Prince of Wales, succeeded to the throne as His Majesty King Edward VIII, Emperor of India.

With the old King's death, Court mourning was ordered for nine months, until 21 October, with half-mourning coming into effect on 21 July. As an immediate mark of national respect, the Law Courts, the Stock Exchange, and all cinemas and theatres were closed; even sporting events were cancelled. At Sandringham, meanwhile, some were already muttering indignantly that the new reign had got off to a bad start, giving as their reason an apparently premature and callous royal command. Ever since the days of King Edward VII, the clocks at Sandringham had been set half an hour fast. Some say this was due to Queen Alexandra's notorious unpunctuality. Whatever the reason, Edward VIII decided that Greenwich Time would henceforth be observed, and his command to send for the clockman was hastened by some unexplained mistake that had occurred because of the discrepancy between Greenwich and Sandringham Time.

'I'll fix those bloody clocks,' the King had declared angrily, and thus the order went out. The effect, Lady Donaldson tells us, 'was horribly offensive and can be explained only by the idea that the Prince was so closely imprisoned in his own personal crisis that he had no thoughts for anyone else'. This may well be true, but who is to say how even a King should conduct himself at such an intensely personal time? Who knows what emotions might prompt an outburst of anger, an unfortunate but 'horribly offensive' order? And if, as Helen Hardinge wrote, the young King's grief was 'frantic and unreasonable', far in excess of that of 'his mother and three brothers', is it really any wonder? Suddenly the whole burden of sovereignty had devolved upon him; suddenly his romance threatened to spark off a true battle royal between the sovereign and the Establishment. It is scarcely surprising, therefore, that a man of Edward VIII's disposition, should overreact at the daunting prospect of things to come.

*

The first of Edward VIII's duties as King was to attend his Accession Council at St James's Palace, on 21 January. That morning, accompanied by his brother and Heir Presumptive, the Duke of York, he flew from Bircham Newton Royal Air Force Aerodrome in Norfolk to Hendon in North London. The King's love of all things novel included the conquest of the air, and despite the consternation of many he became the first British sovereign to travel by aeroplane. It was, in fact, at Edward VIII's instigation that the King's Flight itself (currently the Queen's Flight) was established.

A contemporary newspaper report tells us:

With his sorrow still heavy upon him, King Edward the Eighth took up the reins of monarchy. His first duty was to hold his first Privy Council; here in the following simple words, he declared his determination to work for the happiness of his people:

'Your Royal Highnesses, My Lords and Gentlemen. The irreparable loss which the British Commonwealth of Nations has sustained by the death of His Majesty My Beloved Father, has devolved upon Me the duty of Sovereignty.

'I know how much you and all My Subjects, with I hope I may say the whole world, feel for Me in My sorrow, and I am confident in the affectionate sympathy which will be extended to My Dear Mother in Her overpowering grief.

'When My Father stood here twenty-six years ago He declared that one of the objects of His life would be to uphold Constitutional government. In this I am determined to follow in My Father's footsteps and to work, as He did throughout His life, for the happiness and welfare of all classes of My subjects.

'I place my reliance upon the loyalty and affection of My peoples throughout the Empire, and upon the wisdom of their Parliaments, to support Me in this heavy task, and I pray that God will guide Me to perform it.'

Although the King told his Prime Minister that he had not experienced the overwhelming sensation his father claimed to have felt at his own Accession Council, Stanley Baldwin reported that His Majesty had held his written speech first in one tremulous hand, then in both, and had finally rested the document on the table before him. Clement Attlee noted that the King appeared 'very nervous and ill at ease'.

The following day traditional ceremonies proclaiming Edward VIII's accession took place throughout Britain. In London, the King was proclaimed by Garter King of Arms from a balcony at St James's Palace, looking out across Friary Court to Marlborough House. Royal protocol has never required the sovereign to witness this particular ceremony, but in 1936 Edward VIII decided that he wished to do so. Alongside him, peering intently through the windows, was Mrs Simpson. The caption given to a press photograph at the time spoke of her as 'the King's unknown companion'.

When the royal party left St James's, Wallis thanked the King for arranging for her to be present, adding that she realized how different everything must now be. The King replied that nothing could ever change his feelings towards her. Chips Channon, who had stood in the crowd to watch the Proclamation, wrote in his diary that day: 'It was a fleeting brilliant ceremony. . . . Afterwards I saw a large black car (the King's) drive away, with the blinds pulled half down. The crowd bowed, thinking that it contained the Duchess of Kent, but I saw Mrs Simpson.'

Channon went on: 'We are all riveted by the position of Mrs S—. No man has ever been so in love as the present King; but can she be another Mrs Fitzherbert? [In December 1785, Maria Fitzherbert, a Roman Catholic widow, became the secret wife of the Prince Regent, afterwards King George IV.] If he drops her she will fall – fall – into the nothingness whence she came, but I hope he will not, for she is a good, kindly woman, who has had an excellent influence on the young monarch.'

*

The new King Edward VIII follows his father's coffin to Westminster Hall. On the way, the Maltese cross fell from the Imperial State Crown

The remains of George V were borne from Sandringham to Westminster Hall on 23 January. There the King's coffin was to lie in state until interred at St George's Chapel, Windsor Castle, five days later. On its progress through the streets of London, however, something happened which struck even the unsuperstitious young King as a sign of ill-omen. Traditionally placed on a gun-carriage, the dead monarch's coffin was draped with the Royal Standard, on top of which the bejewelled Imperial State Crown was secured. As the cortège neared Westminster, the King noticed a sudden 'flash of light dancing along the pavement'. Inexplicably the diamond Maltese cross, which surmounts the State Crown, had become dislodged from its setting and had fallen into the road.

Harold Nicolson, who was present at Westminster Hall that day, also saw the portent and remarked upon it in his diary:

Six huge guardsmen carry the coffin which slips quite easily onto the catafalque. The coffin remains there, just a wreath of flowers and the crown, its diamonds winking in the candle-light. It is at that stage that I notice that something has gone wrong with the crown. The Maltese cross at the top is missing. . . . A most terrible omen.

*

Little by little, what Edward VIII called 'the relentless grind of the King's daily life' began to betray his growing distaste for many aspects of his new role. State papers contained in the red leather dispatch boxes delivered to the sovereign every day of the week were at first attended to expediently. Then days, sometimes even weeks, would drift by before they were returned, often without any evidence that the King had even looked at them. More disconcerting, not least because of the security risks involved, was the knowledge that confidential papers were left completely un-attended at Fort Belvedere. Alarmed by the King's negligence, the Foreign Office took the unprecedented step of screening all documents that were to be sent to the Fort.

By now it was becoming increasingly apparent to all who surrounded the King that the only thing that interested him was his relationship with Mrs Simpson. Everything else was irksome and intrusive. 'It was she who filled his thoughts at all times,' wrote Alexander Hardinge, the King's Assistant Private Secretary; 'she alone who mattered, before her the affairs of state sank into insignificance.'

Affairs of state were not alone in suffering from the King's total lack of consideration. Friends of his were summarily dropped in favour of Wallis's; members of his Household grew angry at the inconvenient hours at which he might decide that their services were required. The Duchess of York, to say nothing of the King's domestic staff, took exception to Mrs Simpson's proprietorial manner within the inner sanctums of the King's houses. Servants at Buckingham Palace were outraged when their 'beer money' was cut, and in the King's attempt to make Sandringham and Balmoral more cost-effective, staff were shoddily dismissed, regardless of their length of service or future prospects. Petty-minded acts such as these only served to highlight mounting complaints about the King's arrogance and conceit, while the savings made from his brutal methods of retrench-

Edward VIII returning to
Buckingham Palace after
Trooping the Colour

ment amounted to little or nothing when compared to the thousands of pounds he gladly spent on jewels with which to adorn Mrs Simpson.

In public, however, Edward VIII was still capable of using his extraordinary charm to devastating effect. On Clydeside he was surrounded by dockworkers who cried, 'Good Old Teddy', the familiar greeting synonymous with his grandfather, King Edward VII. In covering that particular visit, one newspaper reported:

The King's first visit as King to the hard-hit area of Clydeside will never be forgotten by those who saw it. He walked for seven miles about the most wonderful ship in the world, the *Queen Mary*, sitting in its armchairs, turning on taps in the cabins, and like a boy, balancing a penny on the edge of the engine to see how smoothly it ran.

And from all the magnificence King Edward passed into the slums from a world of pride and power to the world of human misery of which no man is more ashamed than he. . . .

He went to a blind steelworker's home in which seven people live in a kitchen and a bedroom. In another tenement King Edward went upstairs and found six in one room, and in another he climbed to the top floor and found a five-year-old boy, Charlie Storrie. 'Are you my new King?' asked the boy, and the King shook hands with him and said, 'Yes, sonny; I am your new King.'

And so it went on, the people cheering wildly as he passed among them crying out 'God bless Your Majesty'. Then the King had tea with the Lord Provost and told him that these people should have better homes than the appalling places he had seen. We may imagine that he added that the nation which could build that great ship could also build clean homes for its people.

Duties of a ceremonial nature took the King to France to unveil the Canadian National War Memorial at Vimy Ridge; at St George's Chapel, Windsor Castle, he reviewed a St George's Day rally of one thousand Boy Scouts; he became the second monarch in 250 years to distribute 'alms to the poor', during the Royal Maundy service at Westminster Abbey, and he took the salute at a number of military parades.

It was at the close of one such ceremony – the presentation of new Colours to the Brigade of Guards in Hyde Park on 16 July 1936 – that a startling incident occurred which made banner headlines throughout the Empire next day. The *Cape Times*, to cite just one example, proclaimed: 'Sensational Attempt on Life of The King', and went on to devote its entire front page to news of the event:

Great Britain was shocked by a sensational incident believed to have been an attack on the life of King Edward.

His Majesty at the
Canadian War Memorial.
Vimy Ridge, July 1936

As the King was riding along Constitution Hill after presenting new colours to his Guards a man produced a revolver loaded in four chambers and attempted to level it at His Majesty. A woman in the crowd promptly knocked the gun out of his hand, according to eye-witnesses, and it fell in the roadway near the King's horse. Mad with excitement, the crowd surged round the would-be assassin and flung him to the ground. The police had difficulty in rescuing him.

A striking feature of the incident was the cool self-possession of the King, who looked directly at the man when the incident occurred but rode on apparently with calm indifference.

The King's assailant, a Scotsman named as Jerome Bannigan, alias George Andrew Mahon, was charged at Bow Street Police Court with 'being in possession of a firearm with intent to endanger life'. Although he protested that he had not intended to harm, much less assassinate, the King, Bannigan was remanded in custody and driven away to Brixton Prison.

A bored King acknowledging a line of debutantes at Buckingham Palace, July 1936

As calmly as he had ridden on to Buckingham Palace, the King dismissed the incident. After lunching at York House, he spent the afternoon playing golf at Coombe Hill in Surrey. In the House of Commons, meantime, questions about the attack were put to the Home Secretary, Sir John Simon, and a flood of messages from all over the world, congratulating the King on his escape, poured into St James's Palace. They came from the Emperor of Japan, the Kings of Greece and the Belgians, the Regent of Hungary, Pope Pius XI, the Governor-General of Australia, the Governor-General of New Zealand, and the Prime Minister of Canada. There were messages, too, from Benito Mussolini and Adolf Hitler, whose telegram read: 'I have just received the news of the execrable attempted attack on Your Majesty. I beg to tender to Your Majesty my heartiest congratulations on your escape from this danger.'

One danger from which Edward VIII could not escape, however, was boredom, especially when caused by such events as the presentation of debutantes. Mourning for George V meant that the 'Courts', at which endless lines of young women trotted up to the throne, curtsied to the sovereign, and then disappeared into a great whirl of parties, had to be postponed. In the summer of 1936, therefore, it was decided to dispose of this particular ritual by staging two garden parties at Buckingham Palace, during which some six hundred debutantes would form up in an orderly line and, one by one, move forward to make their curtsies to the King. At the first of these garden parties, Edward VIII, accompanied by the Dukes and Duchesses of York and Kent, Lady Maud Carnegie, and the Marchioness of Carisbrooke, took his place beneath the huge red-and-gold Shamiana durbar canopy, which George V had brought back from India in 1911. It was not long after the eagerly awaited presentations began that boredom glazed the King's features; and when, just over an hour later, it came on to rain, sending the crocodile of young women scuttling for cover, the King decided that enough was enough and strode back across the dank camomile lawn to the Palace, leaving two hundred debutantes to wonder if they would curtsy that day or not. The answer was that they would not. Instead the King instructed the Lord Chamberlain, the Earl of Cromer, to issue a statement which read: 'The Lord Chamberlain is commanded to announce that those ladies summoned to this afternoon's Reception who, owing to the interruption of this ceremony by the weather, were unable to pass the King's presence, will be considered as having been officially presented at Court.'

Some have since criticized the King for not reappearing at the garden party when the rain ceased that afternoon. But of all the retrospective criticism levelled at the way he performed his public engagements as sovereign, the most uncompromising has always appeared to centre upon something he said during his visit to South Wales, less than a month before his abdication. If the King had been appalled by the squalid tenements and pitiful conditions in which the people of Clydeside lived, he was profoundly moved by what he saw in the Rhondda and Monmouth valleys in November 1936. Despair among the unemployed, a great many of whom had been without work for a whole decade, beggared description. Wretchedly poor, undernourished, inadequately housed, dispirited, great hosts of men crowded round the King everywhere he went. He talked earnestly to scores of them, and not one doubted his sincerity for a moment. He visited the vast derelict Bessemer Steel Works, which had once employed nine thousand men. Now hundreds greeted him there amidst the ruins by singing an old Welsh hymn. Turning to one of his party, the King said, 'Something must be done to find them work.'

The following day, he visited a council estate at Pontypool and later, at Blaenavon, he told the Chairman of the Unemployed Men's Committee, 'Something will be done about unemployment.' Here at least the King could speak in the knowledge that the Government was planning to give financial assistance to re-start some of the abandoned works. But it was his earlier remark that has since been severely criticized as nothing more than fine rhetoric, given the fact that Edward VIII had by then already told his Prime Minister, Stanley Baldwin, his mother, Queen Mary, and his three brothers, the Dukes of York, Gloucester, and Kent, of his decision to renounce the throne.

Of course, if the King had foolishly led the men of South Wales to believe that he alone could remedy their plight, then their subsequent sense of betrayal, along with every word of criticism, is entirely justified. But if, as seems much more likely, his words were an understandable cry from the heart, or, as the *Daily Mail* put it, 'a call for action', then the King must surely be judged in a very different, more sympathetic light.

Above The King with unemployed workers in South Wales, November 1936

Below On Clydeside, 1936. The King disembarks from the *Queen Mary*, at the end of his visit to the liner

– 6 –

ABDICATION

A T PRECISELY WHAT POINT in their relationship Edward VIII made up his mind to marry Wallis Simpson may never be known with any certainty. It is, however, generally accepted that he had set his heart on the idea some time during 1934.

The decision made, it has been said that the Prince of Wales, as he still was, intended to tell his father of his determination to take another man's wife as his own, but lacked either the courage or the right opportunity to do so. Had the Prince confronted George V, the course of royal history might well have been diverted with much less ado; and the old King's hope, that nothing would come between his second son, 'Bertie', the Duke of York, his adored granddaughter Princess Elizabeth, and the throne, could have become a reality during the final months of his life. As things stood, George V died confirmed in his sad but prophetic belief that 'David' would 'ruin himself' within twelve months.

Setting hypothesis aside, it would be of greater interest to know how and when Edward VIII first asked Ernest Simpson to allow his wife to divorce him and on what terms, for it would be surprising had some kind of settlement not been agreed between the two men. The responsibility for explaining that point, however, must surely rest with some future historian, once access to the Duke of Windsor's private papers is finally granted. For the time being, we have on record an interesting summary of one interview between the King and Mr Simpson, witnessed by Bernard Rickatson-Hatt, a friend of Ernest's and at that time editor-in-chief of Reuters. Rickatson-Hatt told Walter Monckton, who we shall meet presently, that on one occasion he was at York House with Simpson and the King, when the former turned to His Majesty and declared that Wallis would have to choose between them.

What, asked the cuckolded husband, did the King intend to do about the situation? Did he intend to marry Wallis?

VIVE LE ROI!

A patriotic cartoon in *Punch*. Eleven months later, the journal would depict a very different scene

According to Rickatson-Hatt, the King rose from his chair and said, 'Do you really think that I would be crowned without Wallis by my side?'

Lady Alexandra Metcalfe has said that, if true, the King's remark was totally out of character. It is, of course, quite possible that Rickatson-Hatt's memory was at fault, especially since his meeting with Walter

Monckton did not take place until several years after the Abdication. Yet it can only be supposed from this that the question of what should be done had already arisen on at least one occasion; especially since it is now known that during one heated exchange the King and Ernest Simpson actually came to blows.

Whatever the pattern of events, and regardless of what was or was not said in Bernard Rickatson-Hatt's hearing, the fact remains that Edward VIII requested Ernest Simpson to free his wife from their marriage and, in May 1936, while arranging a dinner party at York House, to which Stanley Baldwin had been invited, the King told Wallis, 'Sooner or later my Prime Minister must meet my future wife.'

Left Lady Yule's steam-yacht, the *Nahlin*

Right The King and Mrs Simpson: intimacy that outraged the Empire

One month later, Mrs Simpson accompanied the King on his now famous cruise along the Dalmatian coast, aboard Lady Yule's steam-yacht, the *Nahlin*. Planned as a purely private holiday, the voyage rapidly became a public royal progress, enjoyed just as much by VIPs as by local people, who gathered everywhere to cheer the British King and his party. In Athens, Edward VIII was greeted by the Greek Prime Minister, General Metaxas; in Istanbul, he had two meetings with Kemal Attaturk; in Bulgaria, he was accompanied on his travels by King Boris, and in

The King and Wallis during their much-publicized holiday cruise along the Dalmatian coast, 1936

Yugoslavia by the Regent, Prince Paul, while in Vienna, the King called upon President Miklas and later received the Chancellor, Doctor Schuschnigg.

The cruise of the *Nahlin* – the King's remarkable informality, the ports put into, the cheers of the adoring crowds, the sunbathing in private coves, and so on – has been described so many times before that a detailed impression of it is no longer vital to our story. What is and always will be of the greatest significance, however, is that throughout that summer interlude the King and Mrs Simpson were so very obviously a pair, so conspicuously 'together', that crowds of delighted locals in Dubrovnik greeted them with the cry, 'Zivila ljubav!' – the Yugoslav equivalent of 'Long live love!'

Seeing the *Nahlin* for the first time, 'trim and gleaming white . . . in a picture-book setting of mountains and sunlit sea', made Wallis appreciate 'as never before the pleasure and power that attended those in the company of a King'. She had already seen, of course, and marvelled at how simply even the King's slightest wish 'seemed always to be translated instantly into the most impressive kind of reality. Trains were held; yachts materialized; the best suites in the finest hotels were flung open; aeroplanes stood waiting.' To these remarks she added with considerable awe: 'it seemed unbelievable that I, Wallis Warfield of Baltimore, Maryland, could be part of this enchanted world. It seemed so incredible that it produced in me a happy and unheeding acceptance.'

Like Lewis Carroll's Alice, Mrs Simpson – who in fact described herself as 'Wallis in Wonderland' – tumbled into her new and extraordinary world quite by chance. Yet while it was true that she enjoyed moving in high places and had expressed an ambition to meet the Prince of Wales, it is extremely difficult to accept the Establishment view of her as a scheming, calculating 'adventuress'. At worst, Wallis's vision of herself in the royal world which, not unnaturally, held her spellbound would appear to have been one of foolish naïveté, rather than anything more calculative. We already know that she did not expect her position as the King's favourite to last for ever and, indeed, she had written to him quite early on: 'Sometimes I think you haven't grown-up where love is concerned and perhaps it's only a boyish passion for surely it lacks the thought for me that a man's love is capable of.'

At that point it is clear that Mrs Simpson tended to treat the King's attention as though it were some kind of fantastic adventure. He needed her, and for as long as it should last she was more than happy to go along with the game, helping him to arrange his life, delighted to do whatever she could to ease his loneliness, responding in kind to his bizarre but infantile love letters – though all the while believing that it was tragic that the King could not 'bring himself to marry without loving'. Even as late as February 1936, Wallis was writing to her Aunt Bessie: 'The English would prefer that he marry a Duke's daughter to one of the mangy foreign Princesses left. However only the years and himself can arrange that for him.' For the time being, and in the words of their own private language, 'WE' (meaning Wallis and Edward) would remain 'the boy' and 'the girl', constantly 'holding tight', 'making drowsy', or making 'enormous ooh', locked in their own small – or 'Eanum' – land of dreams.

✳

From the time of the Abdication, to the intense revival of interest in the couple's story that followed the Duchess of Windsor's death half a century later, one question that has frequently been asked is whether Wallis ever really loved the King. Many doubted it, and for years rumour maintained that the Windsors were dreadfully miserable together. Lady Alexandra Metcalfe, a guest at the royal wedding in 1937, noted in her diary at the time: 'If she occasionally showed a glimmer of softness, took his arm, looked at him as though she loved him, one would warm towards her, but her attitude is so correct. The effect is of a woman unmoved by the infatuated love of a younger man.'

Although much more mature than Edward, Mrs Simpson was, in fact, his junior by two years; but if, as Lady Alexandra observed, Wallis did appear 'unmoved', then it might be argued that it was because she had already become resigned to his total dependence on her, in much the same way that the mother of, say, a backward child has to learn to come to terms with the child's constant demands, while outwardly appearing detached from crippling inner emotions. Many theories could be put forward to explain or counter Lady Alexandra Metcalfe's impressions, but there can surely be very little doubt today that Wallis *did* love the King – though whether she was ever *in* love with him, as he was with her, is a question none but the Duchess of Windsor herself could possibly have answered. What remains clear, however, and there was sufficient evidence of it during their lifetime, is the devotion the couple shared throughout the thirty-five years of their married life. One witness to that devotion was Diana Mosley,

who, in 1980, following the publication of her own biography of the Duchess, wrote to the present author: 'It is so strange that people not only wanted the marriage to be unhappy, but even now pretend that it was.'

*

Although Mrs Simpson – as she disclosed in her book, *The Heart Has Its Reasons* – realized that love had overridden friendship during the summer holiday that she and the then Prince of Wales had taken in 1934, it was not until the end of the *Nahlin*'s voyage, two years later, that her eyes were fully opened to the course her 'happy and unheeding' adventure had taken. By then, though she did not know it, nothing could halt the fatal escalation of a situation which the American and Continental newspapers were already hailing as a royal sensation. Suddenly, the dangers that Wallis hadn't seen before, partly because of her ignorance of the way the British monarchy operated, and partly because the idea of marrying the prince hadn't entered her head, became alarmingly apparent.

Seized by panic and in an attempt to avoid 'disaster' – for Edward as well as for herself – she wrote to the King in September 1936, telling him that she must return to her husband. Although she and Ernest were 'poor and unable to do the attractive things . . . which I must confess I do love and enjoy', she explained, she at least would have security and a 'calm congenial life'. In the same letter, Mrs Simpson went on to say that while she and the King had had 'lovely beautiful times' together, he must now attend to his 'job', 'doing it better and in a more dignified manner each year'.

In response, the King totally disregarded Wallis's fears and merely asked, in his usual child-like manner, why she said 'such hard things to David'. 'You see,' he wrote, 'I do love you so entirely and in every way . . . . Madly tenderly adoringly and with admiration and such confidence.' At that Wallis capitulated and, presumably having dismissed all notions of a reconciliation with Ernest, travelled to Scotland, where she joined the King at Balmoral.

*

Until it became impossible for the British press to remain silent about Edward VIII's relationship with Wallis Simpson, the nation at large remained blissfully unaware of the stories then rampaging throughout the United States and Europe. Yet while nothing – not so much as a whisper –

Wallis Simpson

was to be found in the newspapers at home, it was not long before foreign news stories filtered into Britain and the Dominions, which in turn gave rise to an avalanche of letters from Britons living abroad. By October there was no disguising the fact that the issue had reached a stage where it could no longer be ignored. Returning to Downing Street after taking two months off for the sake of his health, Stanley Baldwin found 'a vast volume of correspondence from British subjects and American citizens of British origin in the United States of America, from some of the Dominions and from this country, all expressing perturbation and uneasiness at what was then appearing in the American press'.

Despite his concern, Baldwin nevertheless proceeded slowly and, indeed, with some reluctance, telling Major Hardinge, who had by now become the King's Private Secretary, that he hoped not to have to intervene until after the coronation, which was set for 12 May 1937, still six months away. Current events, however, demanded expediency, and on 17 October Hardinge appealed to the Prime Minister to see the King and urge him to stop the divorce action which Mrs Simpson had decided to file against her husband. Naturally enough it was felt that, as long as Wallis remained married to Ernest Simpson, the constitutional crisis which threatened to crack over their heads could be averted.

The King agreed to see Baldwin at Fort Belvedere a few days later. Assuring his sovereign that he spoke 'not merely as his Premier and counsellor, but as a friend', the Prime Minister addressed himself forthwith to the question of the 'prevalent rumours' about His Majesty, and the detrimental effect they would have not only upon the peoples of the Empire but on the monarchy itself. 'The importance of the integrity of the Crown', said Baldwin,

was far greater than it had ever been. . . . But while this feeling largely depends on the respect that has grown up in the last three generations for the monarchy, it might not take so long, in face of the kind of criticism to which is was being exposed, to lose that power far more rapidly than it was built up, and once lost, I doubt if anything could restore it.

Baldwin then pointed out some of the dangers that might arise during the statutory six-month period separating the decrees nisi and absolute in the Simpson divorce case. One of his concerns was that 'there might be sides taken and factions grow up . . . when no faction ought ever to exist'.

His Majesty King Edward VIII

The Prime Minister then came to the point and restricted his verbosity to one simple, if blunt, question: 'Must the case really go on?'

The King replied, 'Mr Baldwin, I have no right to interfere with the affairs of an individual. It would be wrong were I to attempt to influence Mrs Simpson just because she happens to be a friend of the King's.'

On that note the audience ended, and the Prime Minister scuttled away, having missed a golden opportunity to ask the King if it was his intention to marry Mrs Simpson once she was free.

The case of *Simpson* v. *Simpson* was heard at Ipswich Assizes on Tuesday 27 October, with the plaintiff suing for divorce on the grounds of her husband's adultery at the Hotel de Paris, in the Berkshire village of Bray. Cited as co-respondent was a woman who gave her name as 'Buttercup Kennedy', an alias which in all probability concealed the true identity of Mary Raffray, whose nickname was, in fact, 'Buttercup'. Mrs Simpson was granted her decree nisi that day and, with the co-operation of the newspaper magnates Lord Beaverbrook and Esmond Harmsworth, son of Lord Rothermere, Chairman of the Newspaper Proprietors' Association, the British press reported the divorce in a straightforward, matter-of-fact way, free of all embellishment.

Just over a fortnight later, media discretion looked set to disintegrate, and the menacing spectre of the constitutional crisis Stanley Baldwin had feared loomed oppressively near. Thus, when the King returned to Fort Belvedere on 13 November, having completed a triumphant visit to the Fleet at Southampton, he was told that a letter from his Private Secretary awaited his urgent attention. Major Hardinge wrote:

As Your Majesty's Private Secretary, I feel it my duty to bring to your notice the following facts which have come to my knowledge, and which I *know* to be accurate.

1. The silence of the British Press on the subject of Your Majesty's friendship with Mrs Simpson is *not* going to be maintained. It is probably only a matter of days before the outburst begins. Judging by the letters from British subjects living in foreign countries where the Press has been outspoken, the effect will be calamitous.

2. The Prime Minister and senior members of the Government are meeting to-day to discuss what action should be taken to deal with the serious situation which is developing. As Your Majesty no doubt knows, the resignation of the Government – an eventuality which can by no means be excluded – would result in Your Majesty having to find someone else capable of forming a government which would receive the support of the present House of Commons. I have reason to know that, in view of the feeling

prevalent among members of the House of Commons of all parties, this is hardly within the bounds of possibility. The only alternative remaining is a dissolution and a General Election, in which Your Majesty's personal affairs would be a chief issue – and I cannot help feeling that even those who would sympathize with Your Majesty as an individual would deeply resent the damage which would inevitably be done to the Crown, the corner-stone on which the whole Empire rests.

If Your Majesty will permit me to say so, there is only one step which holds out any prospect of avoiding this dangerous situation, and that is for Mrs Simpson to go abroad *without further delay*, and I would *beg* Your Majesty to give this proposal your earnest consideration before the position has become irretrievable. Owing to the changing attitude of the Press, the matter has become one of great urgency.

I have the honour, etc., etc.,
Alexander Hardinge

As the sovereign's principal officer, it naturally fell to the Private Secretary to warn the King of any potential crisis facing the Cabinet. Yet while Edward VIII did not question Hardinge's right to send such a letter, his reaction to it was one of anger. That anger, as the King put it himself, arose from the very suggestion that he should send from his realm the woman he intended to marry. Convinced that Hardinge had not written of his own volition, but at the instigation of the Prime Minister, the King decided to dispense with Hardinge's services as go-between – the traditional channel of communication betwixt the sovereign and the premier had always been through the Private Secretary – and called instead upon Walter Monckton. A friend of Edward VIII, Monckton had been Attorney-General to His Majesty in 1932, when he was still Prince of Wales; he had become a King's Counsellor in 1930 and, more latterly, had been constitutional adviser to the Nizam of Hyderabad. It was Monckton who advised the King to delay making any decision over Mrs Simpson until her decree absolute had been granted, and that would not be forthcoming until 27 April. The King's response was to confide that he could not in all conscience go ahead with his coronation in May, knowing in his heart that he intended to marry Wallis. To do so, he said, would be to deceive both the Government and the people.

Then the King told Monckton, 'I am beginning to wonder whether I really am the kind of King they want. Am I not a bit too independent? As you know, my make-up is very different from that of my father. I believe they would prefer someone more like him. Well, there is my brother Bertie.' Here, once more, the King voiced doubts about his suitability to the role in which destiny had cast him. And we return again to the argument that, despite all, Edward VIII had never wanted, and did not want, to be King. Indeed it is not at all unreasonable to suggest that, consciously or unconsciously, he clung to Wallis Simpson because he saw in his love for her a means of escape.

For her part, however, Mrs Simpson was ready to quit Britain the moment she had been shown Alexander Hardinge's letter, but the King firmly countered her insistence to be allowed to leave.

'You'll do no such thing; I won't have it,' he said. 'This letter is an impertinence.' Then he added, 'I intend to see the Prime Minister [and] I shall tell him that if the government is opposed to our marriage . . . I am prepared to go.'

At that, Mrs Simpson burst into tears. 'David,' she wept, 'it is madness to think, let alone talk, of such a thing.'

To her pleas that there must be an alternative to abdication, the King replied defiantly, 'I don't believe there can be, after this. I cannot leave this challenge hanging in the air another day.'

In response to the King's summons, Stanley Baldwin arrived at Buckingham Palace at 6.30 the following evening, 16 November. Coming straight to the point, the King said, 'I understand that you and several members of the Cabinet have some fear of a constitutional crisis developing over my friendship with Mrs Simpson.'

Baldwin replied that that was so, and for the first time the word 'marriage' was brought into their conversation. The Prime Minister advised the King that a marriage with Mrs Simpson, a divorced woman with two husbands still living, would not 'receive the approbation of the country'.

'I pointed out to him,' Baldwin said, 'that the position of the King's wife was different from the position of any other citizen in the country; it was part of the price which the King had to pay. His wife becomes Queen; the Queen becomes the Queen of the country; and, therefore, in the choice of a Queen, the voice of the people must be heard.'

In reply the King told Baldwin that his marriage 'had become an indispensable condition to his continued existence', and went on, 'I want you to be the first to know that I have made up my mind and nothing will alter it. . . . I mean to abdicate to marry Mrs Simpson.'

Startled, Baldwin replied: 'Sir, this is a very grave decision and I am deeply grieved.'

When the Prime Minister had left, the King drove to Marlborough House to dine with Queen Mary and his sister, by now the Princess Royal, whose presence he had specifically requested. One other member of the royal family was also present, his brother Harry's wife, Alice, Duchess of Gloucester. Once dinner was over, the King asked the Duchess to leave the room so that he could talk privately with his mother and sister. It was then that he spoke openly of his love for Wallis Simpson and stated that, despite all opposition, he was determined to marry her.

As the King spoke, the sympathy of both his mother and sister turned to shock and astonishment at the very mention of the word 'abdication'. Edward VIII recalled in his memoirs: 'To my Mother, the Monarchy was something sacred and the Sovereign a personage apart. The word "duty" fell between us.' Ironically, the King, who always maintained that he wanted to avoid splitting the nation and endangering the Empire and the throne, considered that it *was* his duty to surrender his high office, rather than keep it – as he had been urged to do – and risk the consequences.

Though angry and profoundly hurt at what she saw as her son's humiliating dereliction of his birthright, the King's dilemma touched Queen Mary very deeply. The following day she wrote to him: 'As your mother, I must send you a line of true sympathy in the difficult position in which you are placed – I have been thinking of you all day, hoping you are making a wise decision for your future.' That same day at Marlborough House, Queen Mary received Stanley Baldwin; 'instead of standing immobile in the middle distance, silent and majestic', as he wrote later, the Queen 'came trotting across the room *exactly like a puppy dog*; and before I had time to bow, took hold of my hand in both of hers and held it tight. "Well, Prime Minister," she said. "*This* is a pretty kettle of fish!" '

Had Queen Mary received Mrs Simpson and talked with her, as Edward VIII wished, it is conceivable that she might have seen her future daughter-in-law in quite a different light. For Wallis, whose outspokenness at Melton Mowbray a few years earlier had impressed and amused the Prince of Wales, may well have seized the opportunity to explain to his mother that, while she loved the King, she had never schemed to become his wife, much less his Queen. Wallis may even have admitted that the weaknesses of vanity and flattery, together with a hedonistic pursuit of the high life, had finally compromised her, forcing her into a situation from where there now seemed to be no escape. It is true, of course, that as Wallis considered her future, so her thoughts constantly darted around in an attempt to find a solution to the problem; the most obvious being to take herself abroad in the hope that she would be forgotten.

Yet even this idea could never have worked in practice, for apart from the fact that matters had already reached the point of no return – at least so far as the King was concerned – Mrs Simpson would have had to have been utterly ruthless in her attempts to remove him from her life. And if the speed at which she yielded to his blandishments to join him at Balmoral that summer was anything to go by, then she could never have found the strength to resist the King's relentless, and inevitable, chase. Thus it is probably right to assume that, in spite of her feelings for him, Wallis Simpson married Edward VIII simply because there were no alternatives.

Queen Mary, as history relates, never received Mrs Simpson, or 'the Adventuress', as she would always call her. Quite apart from anything else, she was a divorcee. In the words of James Pope-Hennessy, her official biographer, 'Queen Mary's views on divorce were clear and strict: one divorce could seldom or never be justified, and to divorce twice, on any grounds whatever, was to her unthinkable. As for the possibility of a lady, "with two husbands living" marrying her eldest son and becoming Queen Consort, this was out of all question.'

Wallis's status as a divorcee was not the only objection. An equally apparent prejudice was her nationality. During the post-war years Britain's political relations with the United States had been rather less than harmonious, and during the 1920s and 1930s – although the King himself delighted in their company – Americans were generally considered to be phoney, brash, and abrasive. Seen by a great many in Britain as being representative of her country's least attractive features, therefore, it was hardly surprising that 'the King's subjects', as James Pope-Hennessy put it, 'did not relish the idea of a transatlantic successor to Queen Mary on the throne'.

✳

By the time Edward VIII set out on his famous visit to Wales in mid-November, the realization that Wallis could never become Queen – a point which had not, in fact, been insisted upon – must certainly have penetrated even the King's obstinate frame of mind. It was during his absence, however, that a possible alternative was suggested. Esmond

The King and Stanley Baldwin. A cartoon in *Punch* as the Abdication story broke.

PRIME MINISTER: 'All the peoples of your Empire, Sir, sympathize with you most deeply; but they all know – as you yourself must – that the Throne is greater than the man.'

Harmsworth had invited Mrs Simpson to lunch with him at Claridges and after a while asked 'in a matter-of-fact way . . . whether any thought had been given to the idea of a morganatic marriage'.

'The whole idea was so astonishing and so filled with incalculable implications,' Wallis was to write, 'that I could not possibly express any opinion as to its feasibility or desirability. And I frankly told him so.' Nevertheless when, on 20 November, Mrs Simpson and Aunt Bessie joined the King at Fort Belvedere, she raised Harmsworth's proposal. The future Lord Rothermere had, of course, explained that, by contracting a morganatic marriage, Wallis could not share the King's rank; moreover, any children born of the union would be without rights of succession. But, he added, a suitable title for her as the King's wife might be the Duchess of Lancaster.

The response was barely lukewarm, but after Wallis and he had thought it over, the King 'sighed wearily and said, "I'll try anything in the spot I'm in now." '

Put to the Prime Minister, the proposal was predictably dismissed as completely out of the question. Parliament, he said, would never pass the necessary legislation any more than the Dominions would countenance a King with a morganatic wife. So far as Stanley Baldwin was concerned, Edward VIII had only three options open to him. They were: to renounce Mrs Simpson; to marry contrary to the advice of his ministers – who would then resign; or to abdicate.

By this time, although the newspapers were still maintaining an uneasy silence, Mrs Simpson had started to receive a vast amount of 'hate mail', including threats on her life. As a precautionary measure, she left the house she had rented in Cumberland Terrace, Regent's Park, and, with Aunt Bessie, headed for the greater security of Fort Belvedere. There on the evening of 2 December the King told her that the 'gentlemen's agreement' which had kept the press silent had now collapsed, and the next day's papers would be full of the 'royal sensation'.

Without a moment's hesitation Wallis said, 'I'm going to leave. I've stayed here too long. I should have gone when you showed me Hardinge's letter.'

The following morning, confronted by the headlines which finally disclosed what much of the western hemisphere already knew, plans were made to spirit Wallis away to Cannes to the Villa Lou Viei, the home of her good friends and fellow Americans, Herman and Katherine Rogers. To accompany Mrs Simpson on what was actually to prove a nightmare dash through France with the press in hot pursuit, the King had chosen his Lord-in-Waiting, 'Perry' (Lord) Brownlow.

Support for the King, especially among the nation's youth, meanwhile gave rise to a popular movement which the press called 'the King's Party'. In London and even around the Fort in Sunningdale, the people's affection for their King manifested itself in a way that reassured Edward VIII of their continuing loyalty. In the capital, mobile 'royalists' drove through the streets yelling, 'God Save The King From Baldwin', singing the National Anthem and 'For He's a Jolly Good Fellow'. Walls were daubed with the slogan, 'Stand By The King', while outside Buckingham Palace and No. 10 Downing Street cheering crowds waved placards defiantly proclaiming, 'Hands Off Our King: Abdication Means Revolution'.

The people rally to the King's aid

GOD SAVE THE KING

Daily Mirror

Registered at the G.P.O. as a newspaper.   No. 10302   Mon. Dec. 7, 1936   One Penny

45,000,000 DEMAND TO KNOW—

1. **What, justly stated and in detail, is the King's request to his Cabinet?**

2. **What steps were taken to ascertain the views of the people of the Dominions and to explain to them the issues involved in this great crisis?**

3. **Is the British Cabinet prepared to approach the Governments of the Dominions with a frank request that they should reconsider their verdict against the King and consent to a marriage even if it involved new legislation?**

4. **Is the British Cabinet sure beyond doubt that the abdication of Edward VIII would not strike a terrible blow at the greatest institution in the world—our monarchy—and thereby cause irreparable harm?**

5. **Would the abdication of our King mean that he would be EXILED not only from Great Britain but also from every country in his Empire?**

—and Then They Will Judge!

130

Media support for the King: the *Daily Mirror* demands to be heard. 7 December 1936

Despite being urged by his friends to take advantage of such loyal and spontaneous activity, the King decided not to fight. For, as he was later to explain: 'By making a stand for myself, I should have left the scars of a civil war. . . . The price of my marriage under such circumstances would have been the infliction of a grievous wound on the social unity of my native land and on that wider unity that is the Empire.'

If the King wouldn't fight, however, Mrs Simpson, although mentally exhausted and close to despair, hadn't yet resigned herself to the inevitable.

Desperate that he should not abdicate, Wallis wrote to Edward VIII on 6 December, suggesting that he tell Baldwin – whom she was convinced was at the heart of a plot to remove the King from his throne – that he had decided against renouncing the crown and would set aside all ideas of marriage until the autumn of 1937. That way, she argued, their plans – not discounting the morganatic proposal – stood a far better chance of succeeding. Even if the Prime Minister were then to turn against them, the world would know that they had persistently tried to strike a compromise. To go to Baldwin with this new proposal, Wallis continued, would also be to vindicate herself. For, as she confessed, she was terrified that world opinion would forever be against her.

The following day, 7 December, Wallis Simpson tried another tactic; she would issue a formal statement of renunciation. Thus, with the help of Lord Brownlow and Herman Rogers, she prepared the following announcement:

Mrs Simpson throughout the last few weeks has invariably wished to avoid any action or proposal which would hurt or damage His Majesty or the Throne.

Today her attitude is unchanged, and she is willing, if such action would solve the problem, to withdraw from a situation that has been rendered both unhappy and untenable.

That afternoon, Wallis telephoned the King at the Fort to tell him of her decision and to read him the statement. 'At first he was unbelieving, then hurt and angry,' she later wrote. 'The connection, as always, was noisy and uncertain. . . . After I finished there was a long silence. I thought that David in his anger had hung up. Then he said slowly, "Go ahead, if you wish; it won't make any difference." '

With the publication of Mrs Simpson's communiqué, the 'unhappy and untenable' situation was temporarily diffused. But when the Prime Minister sent Wallis's solicitor, Theodore Goddard, to Cannes, in order to ask Mrs Simpson to withdraw her divorce petition, the calm was suddenly broken. Telephoning the King once more, this time to tell him that she had acceded to Goddard's request, Edward VIII declared, 'It's all over. The Instrument of Abdication is already prepared. . . . I will be gone from England within forty-eight hours.'

✻

In the drawing-room at Fort Belvedere on the morning of Thursday 10 December 1936, six copies of the Instrument of Abdication and seven copies of the King's message to Parliament were taken from their red dispatch box and laid on the King's desk, ready for His Majesty's signature. The text of his address ran:

After long and anxious consideration, I have determined to renounce the Throne to which I succeeded on the death of my Father, and I am now communicating this my final and irrevocable decision. Realising as I do the gravity of this step, I can only hope that I shall have the understanding of my people in the decision I have taken and the reasons which have led me to take it.

I will not enter now into my private feelings, but I would beg that it should be remembered that the burden which constantly rests upon the shoulders of a Sovereign is so heavy that it can only be borne in circumstances different from those in which I now find myself.

I conceive that I am not overlooking the duty that rests on me to place in the forefront the public interest when I declare that I am conscious that I can no longer discharge this heavy task with efficiency, or with satisfaction to myself.

At about ten o'clock, the Dukes of York, Gloucester, and Kent arrived at the Fort and, with the King, went immediately into the drawing-room. Recalling that historic occasion more than a decade later, the Duke of Windsor wrote:

as if in harmony with the lifting of the almost intolerable pressure of the last few weeks, the fog which for some days had added to the gloom had also lifted.

Sitting at the desk, with my three brothers watching, I began to sign the documents. . . . It was all quite informal. When I had signed the last document I yielded the chair to my brothers, who in turn appended their signatures as witnesses in their order of precedence. The occasion moved me. Like a swimmer surfacing from a great depth, I left the room and stepped outside, inhaling the fresh morning air.

The Instrument of Abdication read:

I, Edward the Eighth, of Great Britain, Ireland, and the British Dominions beyond the Seas, King, Emperor of India, do hereby declare My irrevocable determination to renounce the Throne for Myself and for My descendants, and My desire that effect should be given to this Instrument of Abdication immediately.

✳

Above Brisk business for
newspaper vendors in
London. 10 December 1936

Right Accurate guesswork:
the front page of the
American *Daily Mirror*,
October 1936

Daily Mail

NORTHCLIFFE HOUSE, LONDON, E.C.4.   Telephone: Central 6000.

11th December, 1936.   346th Day.

THE KING HAS CHOSEN

WE have passed through the most anxious and astounding day in the history of our Empire. At its close no longer did King Edward the Eighth hold the most glorious heritage that ever fell to the lot of a ruler. His "final and irrevocable" abdication fills every heart with an overwhe.ming sense of tragedy. Indeed, the event far transcends man's capacity to realise it and all that it implies.

The King's decision was stated in an historic message, such as no English Sovereign has ever before penned. It was read by the Speaker to a hushed and deeply moved House of Commons. "The burden which constantly rests upon the shoulders of a Sovereign is so heavy that it can only be borne in circumstances different from those in which I now find myself," declared the King.

The voice of contention is stilled as the Empire sadly reflects on its great loss. The King's subjects had hoped against hope that the Throne would for many years be filled by a Sovereign so well equipped to lead a great Empire through the difficult days that lie ahead.

Yet the whole Empire is now aware that King Edward has reached his decision only after heart-searching reflection. As far back as November 16 he informed Mr. Baldwin of his intention to marry Mrs. Simpson and that he was "prepared to go."

"This Heavy Task"

When later his proposal for a morganatic marriage was rejected by the British Government after consultation with the Dominions, the King's determination became unshakable.

To no great figure in history has an issue so momentous presented itself in a form so stark and uncompromising. King Edward was faced by alternatives each awe-inspiring in its implications. He could renounce the Throne or the woman he wished to marry.

The appeals addressed to him from all parts of his loyal Empire he was led by his conscience to reject, deeply though he appreciated the spirit which prompted them. He felt that "I can no longer discharge this heavy task with efficiency or with satisfaction to myself."

Remembering his past inestimable services, both as Prince of Wales and during the few short months he has been our King, our hearts cannot but be heavy as we watch him withdraw, followed by the sympathy and regrets of his former subjects, into private life.

The thanks of the Empire are due to Mr. Baldwin for the efforts he made to persuade the King to remain, and for the unhurried consideration which the whole Cabinet gave to the King's affairs and their splendid conduct throughout the crisis. The country will share the Prime Minister's belief that where he failed no other could have succeeded; but nothing will assuage the universal disappointment that the King was unable to respond to the entreaties not only of Mr. Baldwin but of all his subjects.

Our New Ruler

By the Act of Settlement, and as the King's Message of Abdication makes clear, the Throne devolves on the Sovereign's eldest brother, Albert Frederick Arthur George, the Duke of York, who will probably elect to be known as George VI.

At the Coronation, which, it is understood, will be held as already arranged on May 12, the people will seize the opportunity of demonstrating their loyal and abiding affection for their new monarch.

Throughout the great realms to the governance of which the new King is called there will be an instant rally to his side.

It is a supreme and onerous task which he is suddenly summoned to undertake.

Like his predecessor, he has worked indefatigably for the good of his nation and has, in his own words, "travelled over the vast extent of our Empire." Like his predecessor, again, he saw front-line service in the war, fighting for his country first with the Grand Fleet at Jutland, that "battle of the mist," and then with the Royal Air Force in France.

At his side will sit a gracious and active consort, whose warm interest in social work of all kinds has earned the country's admiration.

In this hour of momentous change, the heart of the nation will go out instinctively to the Queen-Mother. Once more in a period of great national stress she has stood forth as the pattern of high courage and nobility.

Long live the King!

One of the most recent portraits of King Edward in naval uniform.

This happy picture of the Duke and Duchess of York was taken during the Jubilee celebrations in May last year.

"I Have Determined To Renounce The Throne..."

AT 3.35 yesterday afternoon Mr. Baldwin, the Prime Minister, entered the House of Commons. Advancing to the Bar of the House, and bowing, he announced:

"A message from his Majesty the King, Sir, signed by his Majesty's own hand..."

The Prime Minister then bowing twice more presented the message to the Speaker, who read it out as follows:

"After long and anxious consideration I have determined to renounce the Throne to which I succeeded on the death of my father, and I am now communicating this my final and irrevocable decision.

"Realising as I do the gravity of this step, I can only hope that I shall have the understanding of my peoples in the decision I have taken and the reasons which have led me to it.

"I will not enter now into my private feelings, but I would beg that it should be remembered that the burden which constantly rests upon the shoulders of a Sovereign is so heavy that it can only be borne in circumstances different from those in which I now find myself.

"I conceive that I am not overlooking the duty that rests on me to place in the forefront the public interest when I declare that I am conscious that I can no longer discharge this heavy task with efficiency or with satisfaction to myself.

"I have accordingly this morning executed an Instrument of Abdication in the terms following:

"'I, Edward the Eighth, of Great Britain, Ireland, and the British Dominions beyond the Seas, King, Emperor of India, do hereby declare My irrevocable determination to renounce the Throne for Myself and for My descendants, and My desire that effect should be given to this Instrument of Abdication immediately.

"'In token whereof I have hereunto set My hand this tenth day of December nineteen hundred and thirty-six, in the presence of the witnesses whose signatures are subscribed.

(Signed) EDWARD, R.I.'

"My execution of this instrument has been witnessed by my three brothers, Their Royal Highnesses the Duke of York, the Duke of Gloucester, and the Duke of Kent.

"I deeply appreciate the spirit which has actuated the appeals which have been made to me to take a different decision and I have, before reaching my final determination, most fully pondered over them.

"But my mind is made up.

"Moreover further delay cannot but be most injurious to the peoples whom I have tried to serve as Prince of Wales and as King and whose future happiness and prosperity are the constant wish of my heart.

"I take my leave of them in the confident hope that the course which I have thought it right to follow is that which is best for the stability of the Throne and Empire and the happiness of my people.

"I am deeply sensible of the consideration which they have always extended to me both before and after my accession to the Throne and which I know they will extend in full measure to my successor.

"I am most anxious that there should be no delay of any kind in giving effect to the instrument which I have executed and that all necessary steps should be taken immediately to secure that my lawful successor my brother His Royal Highness the Duke of York should ascend the Throne."

The Text Issued Last Night of THE BILL OF ABDICATION

THE text of the Abdication Bill was publis last night. It is as follows:

A BILL to

Give effect to his Majesty's declaration of abdication for purposes connected therewith.

WHEREAS His Majesty by His Royal Message of tenth day of December in this present year has pleased to declare that He is irrevocably determine renounce the Throne for Himself and His descenda and has for that purpose executed the Instrument Abdication set out in the Schedule to this Act, and signified His desire that effect thereto should be g immediately:

And whereas, following upon the communication to Dominions of His Majesty's said declaration and de the Dominion of Canada pursuant to the provisio Section Four of the Statute of Westminster, 1931, requested and consented to the enactment of this and the Commonwealth of Australia, the Dominio New Zealand, and the Union of South Africa have as ted thereto:

Be it therefore enacted by the King's most Excellent Maj by and with the advice and consent of the Lords Spir and Temporal and Commons, in this present Parlia assembled and by the authority of the same, as follow

1... (1) Immediately upon the Royal Assent bei signified to this Act the Instrument of Abdicatio executed by his present Majesty on the tenth day December nineteen hundred and thirty-six set out i the schedule to this Act shall have effect, and thereup his Majesty shall cease to be King and there shall a demise of the Crown and accordingly the member the Royal Family then next in succession to the Thro shall succeed, thereto and to all the rights privileg and dignities thereunto belonging.

(2) His Majesty, his issue, if any, and the descendants of that issue, shall not after his Majest abdication have any right, title or interest in or to succession to the Throne, and Section One of the A of Settlement shall be construed accordingly.

(3) The Royal Marriages Act, 1772, shall not ap to his Majesty after his abdication nor to the issue any, of his Majesty or the descendants of that issue.

2... This Act may be cited as His Majest Declaration of Abdication Act, 1936.

There follows the Schedule of the Bill which repea phrasing of the Instrument of Abdication included King's message printed in this page.

At the Fort the following day, as the King lunched with Winston Churchill, his reign ended as unceremoniously as it had begun, and Prince Albert, Duke of York, ascended the throne as King George VI. That evening, the ex-monarch, who briefly reverted to his boyhood title, 'His Royal Highness Prince Edward', dined with members of his family at Royal Lodge, the country home of the new King and Queen, in Windsor Great Park. Those present were King George VI himself (his consort, Queen Elizabeth, was confined to bed at her house in London, suffering from influenza), Queen Mary, the Dukes of Gloucester and Kent, the Princess Royal, Princess Alice, Countess of Athlone, and the Earl of Athlone.

After dinner, Prince Edward was collected by Walter Monckton, who drove him the short distance to Windsor Castle, from where he broadcast his farewell message to the Empire. This is what he said:

At long last I am able to say a few words of my own. I have never wanted to withhold anything, but until now it has been not constitutionally possible for me to speak.

A few hours ago I discharged my last duty as King and Emperor, and now that I have been succeeded by my brother, the Duke of York, my first words must be to declare my allegiance to him. This I do with all my heart.

You all know the reasons which have impelled me to renounce the throne. But I want you to understand that in making up my mind I did not forget the country or the Empire which as Prince of Wales, and lately as King, I have for twenty-five years tried to serve. But you must believe me when I tell you that I have found it impossible to carry the heavy burden of responsibility and to discharge my duties as King as I would wish to do without the help and support of the woman I love.

And I want you to know that the decision I have made has been mine and mine alone. This was a thing I had to judge entirely for myself. The other person most concerned has tried up to the last to persuade me to take a different course. I have made this, the most serious decision of my life, upon a single thought of what would in the end be the best for all.

This decision has been made less difficult to me by the sure knowledge that my brother, with his long training in the public affairs of this country and with his fine qualities, will be able to take my place forthwith, without interruption or injury to the life and progress of the Empire. And he has one matchless blessing, enjoyed by so many of you and not bestowed on me — a happy home with his wife and children.

During these hard days I have been comforted by my Mother and by my Family. The Ministers of the Crown, and in particular Mr Baldwin, the Prime Minister, have always treated me with full consideration. There has never been any constitutional difference between me and them and between me and Parliament. Bred in the constitutional tradition by my Father, I should never have allowed any such issue to arise.

Newspaper coverage of the
King's act. The *Daily Mail*,
11 December 1936

Ever since I was Prince of Wales, and later on when I occupied the throne, I have been treated with the greatest kindness by all classes, wherever I have lived or journeyed throughout the Empire. For that I am very grateful.

I now quit altogether public affairs, and I lay down my burden. It may be some time before I return to my native land, but I shall always follow the fortunes of the British race and Empire with profound interest, and if at any time in the future I can be found of service to His Majesty in a private station I shall not fail. And now we all have a new King. I wish him, and you, his people, happiness and prosperity with all my heart. God bless you all. God Save the King.

*

At the Villa Lou Viei in Cannes, 'the other person most concerned' lay weeping on a sofa, her hands covering her face, as she listened to the broadcast. When it had finished, her friends the Rogerses and their staff tactfully left the room, allowing Mrs Simpson to regain her composure. At Royal Lodge members of the former King's family listened, no doubt experiencing a host of conflicting emotions. But when Prince Edward rejoined them, he felt that what he had said 'had to some extent eased the tension between us'.

Presently, as Queen Mary noted in her journal, 'came the dreadful good-bye as he was leaving that evening for Austria. The whole thing was too pathetic for words.'

At midnight Prince Edward bade farewell to his brothers, and as he bowed to the new King, the Duke of Kent shook his head in disbelief and cried out, 'It isn't possible! It isn't happening!' Minutes later, 'David' drove off through the night, across the Hartford Bridge Flats to Portsmouth, where the destroyer HMS *Fury* waited to ferry him across the Channel.

7

THE DUKE AND
DUCHESS OF WINDSOR

ON THE DAY Edward VIII ceased to be King, his successor, George VI, visited him at the Fort to tell him that as the first act of his reign he intended to bestow upon him a dukedom. King George asked, 'How about the family name of Windsor?'

With evident pleasure Prince Edward murmured the words 'Duke of Windsor' to himself, and the matter of a title for the ex-sovereign was immediately settled.

The following morning, as HMS *Fury* sailed towards France, King George VI announced at his Accession Council that, although his father had adopted 'Windsor' as the name of the Royal House in 1917, a royal dukedom had never been so called. Thus decreed, the former King changed his name for the sixth and last time. Born Prince Edward of York, he had become successively Prince Edward of Cornwall and York, Prince Edward of Wales, Duke of Cornwall, Prince of Wales, King Edward VIII, and now Duke of Windsor.

King George's act of fraternal consideration was not widely reflected elsewhere within the British Establishment. Indeed, with knives drawn, those in high places lost no time in attacking the Duke of Windsor the moment his back was turned. Perhaps the most indefensible of all was the attack made upon him by Cosmo Gordon Lang, Archbishop of Canterbury, who, to quote the late Lord Kinross, 'uttered words of condemnation which seemed, in the ears of a large congregation of listeners, to fall sadly short of those precepts of Christian charity to which his Church aspired'. On Sunday 13 December, this most malevolent of clergymen declared:

Strange and sad it must be that for such a motive, however strongly it pressed upon his heart, he should have disappointed hopes so high, and abandoned a trust so great. Even more strange and sad it is that he should have sought his happiness in a manner

The new King: George VI with Queen Elizabeth, photographed when they were the Duke and Duchess of York

inconsistent with the Christian principles of marriage, and within a social circle whose standards and ways of life are alien to all the best instincts and traditions of his people. Let those who belong to this circle know that today they stand rebuked by the judgement of the nation which had loved King Edward. I have shrunk from saying these words. But I have felt compelled for the sake of sincerity and truth to say them.

Yet for one who has known him since childhood, who has felt his charm and admired his gifts, these words cannot be the last. How can we forget the high hopes and promise of his youth; his most genuine care for the poor, the suffering, the unemployed; his years of eager service both at home and beyond the seas? It is the remembrance of these things that wrings from our heart the cry – 'the pity of it, O, the pity of it'.

Archbishop Lang's broadcast achieved nothing, save to bring down on his head a torrent of outrage and abuse, though it did move Gerald Bullett to compose a short poem, which knew wide circulation:

> My Lord Archbishop, what a scold you are!
> And when your man is down how bold you are!
> Of charity how oddly scant you are!
> How Lang, O Lord, how full of Cantuar!

Doctrinal humbug from the Church was of course no more surprising then than it would be today, but the Primate's sanctimonious moralizing was made yet more unpalatable because of its clear disregard for human weakness. Moreover, there is an amusing and supremely ironic twist to the Church's unremitting attitude towards divorce, when we remember that the very foundation of the Church of England itself hinged on precisely that issue. But for Rome's refusal to sanction the dissolution of Henry VIII's marriage to Catherine of Aragon, Britain's ecclesiastical history might well have told a very different story.

✻

As he left England the Duke of Windsor knew, in his own words, that 'the drawbridges were going up behind me'. Even so, he cannot have guessed the extent to which his own family would ostracize him. In her unpublished memoirs, Lady Iris Mountbatten (the only child of 'Drino', Marquess of Carisbrooke, son of Queen Victoria's youngest daughter Beatrice, Princess Henry of Battenberg) recalled:

The finality with which David . . . disappeared out of thoughts and even memories was shocking. I almost expected that when I mentioned him, I would receive the reply, 'Who?'

Aunt May [Queen Mary] . . . actually seemed unchanged by the great loss of her eldest son. I could see no outward sign that she had been tormented by heartbreak. Her attitude seemed simply to be, 'I do not see how anyone can expect me to understand or accept this.' . . . I think this was the emotion that shocked me most in those around me, they *did* not, *would* not, *could* not allow themselves to begin to understand or think with compassion.

It brought home to me a sense that I had always had, that my family was not motivated by love or human emotions.

✻

If the question of a new title for the former King had been agreed with ease, the matter of a financial settlement was to prove extremely troublesome. As Prince of Wales, Edward VIII had amassed a minimum private fortune of some £800,000 (the equivalent of £20 million today) from the tax-free revenues of the Duchy of Cornwall, to which the Heir Apparent is entitled. Upon the death of his father, Edward VIII also inherited a life interest in Balmoral and Sandringham, since both are the sovereign's private property. This meant that, even after he had abdicated, the Duke of Windsor was entitled to retain that life interest in both estates, which was valued at somewhere in the region of £250,000 (roughly £6 million in today's currency).

During a long meeting between the outgoing and incoming monarchs and their advisers at the Fort on 10 December 1936, it was agreed that Edward VIII would surrender Sandringham and Balmoral to George VI in return for an annuity of £25,000 (the equivalent of £600,000 today). The Government, however, declined to append that allowance to the Civil List, which meant that it became payable from George VI's private funds.

In his book *Kings, Queens and Courtiers*, Kenneth Rose tells us:

That hasty agreement was subsequently altered in two ways, both to the Duke's disadvantage. He was required to bear part of the cost of pensions paid to retired retainers on the Sandringham and Balmoral estates, thereby reducing his allowance from £25,000 to £21,000. And the Government, although contributing nothing directly to the Duke's annuity, persuaded the King to attach a condition to its payment: that until further notice the Duke must not return to England without express permission. If the King did not comply, it was hinted, Parliament might be less generous than otherwise in fixing his own Civil List. Since no condition had been imposed at the time of the Abdication, the Duke felt aggrieved. In an acrimonious exchange of letters, he threatened not only to have King George and his family evicted from Sandringham and

Balmoral as trespassers, but also to lay claim to other valuable royal posses-
sions. . . . He was at length obliged to accept the altered terms of the settlement, but
resentment lingered.

For the rest of his life, the Duke of Windsor would resent the treatment he
and the Duchess received at the hands of the royal family; but, in the winter
of 1936 at least, few thoughts besides the prospect of being reunited with
Mrs Simpson filled his mind.

As we saw earlier, the Duke travelled through France to Austria on the
first leg of his journey into exile, arriving in Vienna on 14 December. For
more than three months, in an agony of anticipation and suspense, the
Duke of Windsor – attended by his devoted friend and equerry, Major
Edward 'Fruity' Metcalfe – stayed at Schloss Enzesfeld, the home of Baron
and Baroness Eugene de Rothschild, before moving on to an hotel near
Ischl.

That the Duke and Wallis were forced to stay apart for so long after the
Abdication – she in France, he in Austria – was a condition imposed by the
divorce laws of that time. For them to have met before 27 April 1937, when
Mrs Simpson's decree absolute was to be granted, would have meant
risking the intervention of the King's Proctor, that 'guardian of public
morals', as he has often been described, and the withholding of the
long-awaited divorce.

To while away his endless days, the Duke went skiing, spent whole
mornings in Turkish baths, attended parties, played poker, went on
shopping expeditions and, of course, spent hours talking to Wallis on the
telephone. There were family visits, too, from the Princess Royal and
Prince George, which, to the Duke's immense satisfaction, attracted the
eager attention of the world press. Eventually the long wait was over and,
on the day that Mrs Simpson received her divorce, the Duke of Windsor set
off for France.

In March of that new year, 1937, Wallis Simpson accepted the offer of a
French-born naturalized American, Charles Bedaux, to stay at his house,
the Château de Candé, in Touraine, near Tours. Neither she nor the Duke
knew Bedaux, whose fortune had been made through a system of industrial
efficiency rather akin to the time-and-motion formula, but Herman Rogers
had met him a few times and it was through him that Bedaux and his wife,
Fern, extended their invitation. Later on, the undesirability of Bedaux's
hospitality became only too apparent. For now, however, there were no

Reunited at the end of their separation. The Duke of Windsor and Mrs Simpson at Candé, France

dark clouds to blight the Duke of Windsor's joy as, at precisely 1.30 p.m. on 4 May, he arrived at Candé.

Writing at the time, the journalist Walter G. Farr, reported: 'We saw the Duke of Windsor wave his hand and smile as a big black limousine shot through the gates . . . a moment later he and Mrs Simpson were kissing on the stone steps of the house.'

'Darling, it's been so long,' the Duke said. 'I can hardly believe that this is you, and I'm here.'

Preparations for the wedding were already in hand by the time the Duke and Mrs Simpson were reunited. There was little to be settled, save the date. It has been said that Wallis, superstitiously heeding the rhyme 'Marry in May and rue the day', had decided on early June. That may well be true, but there were other considerations to be taken into account. Chief among them was the Duke's own decision to wait until after all the celebrations attending his brother's coronation on 12 May had died down. The date finally chosen was Thursday 3 June, sixteen days before Wallis's forty-first birthday and twenty days before the Duke's forty-third. Had he lived longer, it would also have been King George V's seventy-second birthday.

*

On the eve of the wedding, Walter Monckton arrived at the château, a welcome guest but the bearer of news which stunned and outraged the Duke. In a letter from the King, which Monckton had brought from London, George VI told his brother that by his abdication he had placed himself outside the royal line of succession and was therefore no longer entitled to the style of Royal Highness. But, the King went on, it was his wish that the Duke should continue to enjoy the title. To ensure it, he had declared by Letters Patent under the Great Seal – in essence on the advice of his ministers – 'that the Duke of Windsor shall . . . be entitled to hold and enjoy for himself only the title, style or attribute of Royal Highness, so however that his wife and descendants, if any, shall not hold the same title or attribute'.

That the Duchess-to-be was never to share her husband's royal status balanced purely on the argument that, since she had already divorced two husbands, she might one day dispose of her third in the same manner; were that possibility ever to be realized, nothing could deprive Wallis of the title 'Royal Highness'. Yet it is nevertheless difficult to understand why George VI was under the impression that, by renouncing the throne, his brother had forfeited the title that was rightfully his from birth. It simply could not be. On the premise of 'once a Royal Highness always a Royal Highness', all the King had formally to create by Letters Patent under the Great Seal was the dukedom of Windsor. Indeed, it was by the King's express command that Sir John Reith, Director-General of the BBC, had announced the former King as 'His Royal Highness Prince Edward' on the night he broadcast his farewell speech to the Empire. This implies that George VI was well aware of his brother's rightful title.

Hurt by the King's message, the Duke of Windsor declared in disbelief and anger, 'I know Bertie – I know he couldn't have written this letter on his own. Why in God's name would they do this to me at this time!'

Opinions concerning the legality of the King's action vary to this day. But at the time Sir William Jowitt, KC (who became Lord Chancellor in the Labour Government of 1945), was certainly among those who considered it illegal.

Recalling his unpleasant mission at Candé, Walter Monckton wrote: 'When I arrived [the Duke] received the news almost in the same words his brother had used when he sent me off. "This is a nice wedding present".' Sympathizing with his former sovereign, Monckton went on:

When he had been King he was told that he could not marry Mrs Simpson because she would have to take his status and be Queen, so he gave up his Kingdom and Empire to make her his wife. He could not give up his royal birth, or his right to be called 'His Royal Highness' which flowed from it. It was a little hard to be told, when he did marry her, that she would not have the same status as himself.

The irony of the Crown's vendetta was that the Duchess of Windsor was placed in exactly the same position as if a morganatic marriage had been permitted. To the Duchess herself, the title of Royal Highness represented the difference between having personal dignity restored and living as an outcast. To the Duke it meant seeing his wife – like the wives of his brothers – properly accepted as a member of the royal family. That she never was soured his life.

*

But to return now to Candé where, by the evening of 2 June 1937, all was prepared for the day ahead. Cecil Beaton had taken the formal photographs of the bridal couple in their wedding finery; as her gift to the bride, Constance Spry had provided all the floral decorations, including magnificent pedestal arrangements of lilies and white peonies; and the Reverend Robert Anderson Jardine, vicar of St Paul's Church, Darlington, who had offered to marry the royal couple in defiance of his bishop's order to the contrary, had conducted the principal figures through a rehearsal of the wedding ceremony.

In the salon of the château at 11.35 the following morning, the Mayor of Monts, Dr Mercier, opened the obligatory civil ceremony and exactly twelve minutes later pronounced the Duke and his bride 'united in the bonds of matrimony'. In a somewhat fulsome speech to the bridal pair, the Mayor then said:

By one of those caprices in which fate delights, it is under the blue skies and amidst the flowers of the garden of France, on the banks of the Indre, that the most moving of idylls has blossomed. Behind the green leaves of the ancient park of the discreet Château de Candé, in a setting which Dr and Mrs Bedaux could not have prepared better had they foreseen the great event which was to take place, the illustrious union which many hearts will secretly celebrate today has as officiating officer the mayor of a little village of Touraine. He would feel himself unworthy of the great honour which falls to him had he not the feeling, in fulfilling the rites in accordance with the laws of his country, that in this simple but solemn ceremony he represents a nation which has always been sensitive to the charm and chivalrous unselfishness and bold gestures prompted by the dictates of the heart. . . .

Your Royal Highness, Duchess, we are happy in your happiness.

The signatures of all those who attended the Windsors' wedding on 3 June 1937

Left The Duchess of
Windsor on her wedding-
day with Sir Walter
Monckton

Right The bride pouring tea
for the bridegroom,
watched by the bestman,
Major Metcalfe

Then came the religious service that the Duke had so earnestly desired.
The guests – who included Wallis's Aunt Bessie Merryman, Lady Alexandra Metcalfe, Randolph Churchill, Walter Monckton, Charles and Fern
Bedaux, and Lady Selby, who represented her husband, Sir Walford –
assembled in the music room shortly before midday. After a few minutes
the bridegroom entered with 'Fruity' Metcalfe, whom he had asked to act
as best man when it became clear that none of his brothers dared to be.
Moments later came the bride, escorted by Herman Rogers. For her
wedding Wallis, who married the Duke not as Mrs Simpson but as Mrs
Warfield (she had reverted to her maiden name by deed poll less than a
month earlier), wore a long dress of soft blue crêpe satin with a short,
tight-fitting jacket, and a hat of tiny feathers trimmed with a tulle 'halo'.
On her right wrist she wore the Duke's wedding present, a sapphire and
diamond bracelet, three inches deep, and at her throat a brooch to match.

In her diary that afternoon, Lady Alexandra Metcalfe wrote:

It's over & it's true. I felt all through the ceremony that I must be in a dream. It was
hard not to cry & in fact I did.

June 1937. The Duke of
Windsor and his bride at
the Château de Candé.
A formal wedding portrait
by Cecil Beaton

Jardine read the service simply & well.... His responses were clear & very well said.... Her voice ... lower but clear. It could be nothing but pitiable & tragic to see a King of England of only 6 months ago, an idolized King, married under those circumstances, & yet pathetic as it was, his manner was so simple and dignified & he was so sure of himself in his happiness that it gave something to the sad little service which it is hard to describe. He had tears running down his face when he came into the salon after the ceremony. She also could not have done it better.

At three minutes past six that evening, the Duke and Duchess of Windsor, cheered by a crowd of five thousand, left Candé at the start of a six-hour, 200-mile car journey to Laroche-Mijelle. One journalist reported in a contemporary newspaper report: 'The Duke and Duchess took two bunches of red roses with them when they left the château. All along the road across the Touraine, villagers and townsfolk turned out to greet them, and each time they passed a cheering crowd the Duchess took a rose and flung it through the window of the car as a token of gratitude.'

The Windsors cheered by local people at the start of their honeymoon

Shortly after midnight the Windsors boarded the Simplon Express *en route* to Carinthia in Southern Austria and their honeymoon destination, the Castle Wasserleonburg. Overlooking Lake Worthesee, the castle had been put at the Duke and Duchess's disposal by its owner, Count Paul Münster.

At home in Britain, the royal family's interest in the Duke of Windsor's wedding was, at best, muted. In the circumstances, of course, this was not surprising. But while they doubtless heard the marriage announced in a fifty-five-word statement, included in the BBC's regular news bulletins, King George and Queen Elizabeth, along with the Duke and Duchess of Kent, were curious to know more. Thus when they met Major and Lady Alexandra Metcalfe shortly after their return to England, they asked to hear all about the wedding. Once told, the subject was never mentioned again.

In the meantime, the Duke and Duchess of Windsor were enjoying their three-month honeymoon. From their lakeside base at Wasserleonburg they took short trips around Austria and across the border into Hungary and Czechoslovakia. At the end of July they extended their travels to include a much-publicized holiday in Venice, and in September decided to move on to Paris. There while searching for a house of their own, they took a small suite at the Hôtel Meurice, overlooking the gardens of the Tuileries. Very soon they found the Château de la Maye, a part-furnished house near Versailles, but after a few months accepted the offer of long leases on two alternative houses – one in Paris, No. 24 Boulevard Suchet, the other a villa at Cap d'Antibes, known as la Croë.

During all their years in Paris, the Duke and Duchess never bought a house of their own. This, at least in the early years, was because the Duke believed that when his wife was accorded royal style and was formally received, if only once, by the King and Queen, they would return to England to live privately at Fort Belvedere. Indeed, as Duke of York, George VI had promised Walter Monckton that the Fort would be reserved for the Duke, so that after a suitable interlude he and the Duchess would have a house to come back to. As we know, the Windsors never made a permanent return – in life anyway – and for twenty years the Fort remained uninhabited. Locked up, shuttered, and pushed from the royal family's mind as being a part of history best forgotten, the house was left to decay until 1956. In that year, the Honourable Gerald Lascelles, first cousin to the present Queen, and both nephew and godson of the Duke of Windsor,

took the Fort on. He and his first wife, the former Angela Dowding, faced the formidable task of restoring the house and grounds – ruined not only by neglect, but also by vandals – to their former beauty. The Duke of Windsor never lost his love for the Fort and until 1976, when it passed out of the royal family's ownership, he continued to take the keenest interest in it.

The question of housing – though of an altogether more humble kind – was one of the reasons which led the Duke and Duchess of Windsor to visit Nazi Germany in the autumn of 1937. And it is at this point that Charles Bedaux, the owner of the Château de Candé, briefly re-enters our story.

The Duke and Duchess of Windsor at la Croë, their villa on the Riviera

Visiting Nazi Germany. The Duke and Duchess with the notorious Dr Ley, October 1937

During their fleeting friendship, Bedaux discovered that he and the Duke of Windsor shared an interest in labour conditions and the working man. It was to transpire, however, that the Duke's interest, motivated by the most altruistic of reasons, ran contrary to Bedaux's. The latter's concern was of a purely commercial nature, extending no further than personal gain; in short, to what he could make out of what the American trade union the COI called 'one of the most completely exhausting, inhuman "efficiency" systems ever invented'. Quoting the American writer Janet Flanner, Lady Donaldson tells us that Bedaux thought of himself as 'an industrial saviour', who wanted 'his ideas and methods to dominate the workings of an organization long after his engineers had gone on to another task'.

In Germany, however, Bedaux's methods had come unstuck when, in 1933, his enterprise was suppressed by the Nazis because it conflicted with their 'Strength through Joy' movement. Not until 1937, while he was still basking in the reflected glory of the royal wedding, was Bedaux told that he could reopen his business, on condition that he paid the Nazi authorities $50,000 US and that he agreed to hand over to the notorious Dr Robert Ley, leader of the German Labour Front, a permanent cut of his business profits.

To Bedaux, the Duke of Windsor, with his almost lifelong pro-German sympathies – to say nothing of their long-term political possibilities – must have seemed a godsend. Unsuspecting that he was to be used as a pawn in an insidious game, the Duke proved a willing victim. So inspired was he, in fact, and so convinced that he could put his knowledge to good use, that he even planned to follow his German tour with a visit to the United States, in order to study labour conditions there.

Upon their arrival in Berlin on 11 October, the Duke and Duchess were welcomed by Dr Ley himself. The British Embassy sent only the Third Secretary. The Ambassador, Sir Neville Henderson, had 'unexpectedly' left the German capital, while Sir George Ogilvie Forbes, the Chargé d'Affaires, had been directed 'to take no official cognizance' of the visit. Guided by Ley, the Windsors were taken to see working people's houses, hospitals, and youth centres in Dresden, Nuremburg, Stuttgart, and Munich – the Duke carefully restricting his conversation, all the while, to the reasons for his tour.

At Berchtesgaden, on the last day of the visit, having already met Göring, Himmler, Hess, and Goebbels, the Duke and Duchess were received by the Führer himself. Of their meeting, Hitler's interpreter, Dr Paul Schmidt, wrote:

Hitler was evidently making an effort to be as amiable as possible towards the Duke, whom he regarded as Germany's friend. . . . In these conversations there was, so far as I could see, nothing whatever to indicate whether the Duke of Windsor really sympathized with the ideology and practices of the Third Reich, as Hitler seemed to assume he did. Apart from some appreciative words for the measures taken in Germany in the field of social welfare the Duke did not discuss political questions.

Nevertheless in Britain and America, the Windsors' visit gave rise to a great deal of anger and indignation. Writing in the socialist newspaper *Forward*, Herbert Morrison, Labour MP and leader of the then London County Council, said:

The choice before the ex-King is either to fade out from the public eye or to be a nuisance. It is a hard choice, perhaps, for one of his temperament, but the Duke of Windsor would be wise to fade out. . . .

If the Duke wants to study social problems he had far better quietly read books and get advice in private, rather than 'put his foot into it' in this way.

Almost at the eleventh hour the Windsors cancelled their proposed American tour. An official statement from Paris, issued on behalf of the Duke, said:

His Royal Highness arrived at his decision . . . with great reluctance and after much deliberation, but he feels that owing to the grave misconceptions which have arisen and the misstatements which have appeared in regard to the motives and purpose of his industrial tour, there is no alternative but to defer it. . . .

The Duke emphatically repeats that there is no shadow of justification for any suggestion that he is allied to any industrial system or that he is for or against any political or racial doctrine, and he expresses his earnest hope that after this announcement his real sincere motive for the proposed visit to America will be properly understood.

8

IN EXILE

LESS THAN TWO YEARS later, with the outbreak of the Second World War in September 1939, one of the questions that faced King George VI and the Prime Minister Neville Chamberlain was what was to be done about the Windsors. It was already perfectly clear that the Queen (the present Queen Mother), who despised the Duchess and bitterly resented the Duke, was vehemently opposed to their return. At length, Chamberlain directed that the Duke and his wife should be allowed to come to Britain only if he was prepared to accept one of two posts. The first was an Assistant Regional Commissioner for Wales, with responsibility for civil defence; the second was as Liaison Officer with the British Military Mission at the French General Headquarters at Vincennes.

Given that the Duke now hoped the moment had come when he could re-establish himself as a prince in his own country, he naturally chose the first appointment. Then quite suddenly, although he was no doubt pushed into it by Queen Elizabeth, George VI decided that his brother would be more usefully employed with the British Mission in France. Since the Duke and Duchess had only just set foot in England – having been collected from Cherbourg at Winston Churchill's behest by HMS *Kelly*, under the command of Lord Louis Mountbatten – this farcical turn of events looked like some kind of ghastly practical joke. Nevertheless the Duke of Windsor, who for this appointment was temporarily demoted in rank from Field Marshal to Major-General, packed his bags and returned with the Duchess whence he had come.

For the time being, rather than open up their house on the Boulevard Suchet, the Windsors stayed at the Trianon Palace Hotel in Versailles, where the Duchess occupied herself with a group which called itself Les Colis du Trianon. This organization, which made comforts for the troops, had been started by the Duchess's friend Lady Mendl, who in peacetime enjoyed a considerable reputation as an interior decorator. The Windsors

A brief return to England, 1939

were often guests of Elsie Mendl and her husband Sir Charles at their house near the Petit Trianon; and in her biography of the Duchess, Diana Mosley recounts an amusing incident which occurred there one evening during the period known as 'the phoney war'. Lady Mosley tells us:

The Duke was away with the army. The Duchess was playing backgammon with Noël

Major-General HRH The Duke of Windsor on the Western Front, 1940

Coward when the butler approached and said quietly, 'Your Grace, His Royal Highness on the telephone.' The Duchess, absorbed in her game, did not hear. The butler spoke a little louder. 'Your Royal Highness, His Royal Highness on the telephone.' As she still paid no attention the butler almost shouted, 'Your Majesty, His Royal Highness on the telephone.' The Duchess got up to follow him, saying to her companions as she did so: 'He's never heard what happened.'

✲

In his role as Liaison Officer with the British Mission, a job which has sometimes been called menial, the Duke of Windsor rendered the Army a service of considerable importance. All through the winter of 1939, the French High Command, suspicious of its allies, had forbidden 'foreign' visits to the Maginot Line – that is, until the popular Prince de Galles of the First World War arrived. Then the French attitude warmed completely, and the Duke was permitted to go wherever he wished. The outcome was that he found himself in a perfect position to discover weak links in the defence chain and report on them accordingly. This he did with invaluable precision, with the result that Major-General Howard Vyse commended the Duke's work to the War Office in London.

With the fall of France in 1940, the Duke and Duchess of Windsor crossed into neutral Spain, thence to Portugal. Once more the question of what should be done with them had to be considered. Like his predecessor, Winston Churchill, now elected to the premiership, directed that the couple must return to England and arranged for two flying-boats to pick them up. From Lisbon, however, the Duke of Windsor cabled his old friend Churchill that he wouldn't move an inch unless two conditions were met. Inevitably both concerned Wallis's standing as his wife. Once again the Duke stipulated that the Duchess should be created a Royal Highness, and that the King and Queen should receive them. The point of such a meeting was simply that it would be recorded in the Court Circular – published in *The Times* and the *Daily Telegraph* – and, to all intents and purposes, the cloud of disgrace under which the Windsors had lived ever since the Abdication would be dispelled.

Churchill, faced with a recalcitrant ex-King, whose presence in a foreign state was potentially extremely dangerous, had no choice but to employ strong-arm tactics. Unless Major-General the Duke of Windsor returned to England forthwith, the Prime Minister advised, he would be court-

The Governor and his Lady.
The Duke and Duchess of Windsor
in the Bahamas, 1943

martialled. In the event this threat was superseded by the Duke's appointment to the Governorship of the Bahamas.

It has been argued that the Duke's stance at this time was as small-minded as that adopted by 'the Establishment' over the Duchess of Windsor's status. Perhaps it was, but it must be remembered that the Duke's anger at the insult he considered to have been delivered on the eve of his wedding hardened his resolve to do anything which might restore his wife's 'dignity'.

At that time, although it was only discovered much later when German documents were captured, a bizarre plot had been hatched by Ribbentrop, the Nazi Foreign Minister, to hold the Duke of Windsor in Spain, not only for the purpose of undermining British morale but, should the opportunity have ever arisen, to oust George VI and reinstate Edward VIII as a puppet king. It seems highly unlikely that the Duke ever gave the Nazis the slightest encouragement in their fiendish scheme, but there remained some doubt none the less. Those who knew the Duke well naturally defended his honour and fiercely maintained that neither he nor the Duchess would ever have been party to any such plans. Be that as it may, the Duke of Windsor had exhibited an appalling lack of discretion in voicing his opinion that Britain would probably be defeated by the Nazis, particularly since he did so in the hearing of German officials. He did make it plain, however, that were Britain to be beaten, he would help to negotiate peace only if asked to do so by the British Government.

Whatever plans Germany may have had for the Windsors were thwarted when the Duke and Duchess set sail for the Bahamas in August 1940. A chain of islands which form a continuation of the Florida cays, the Bahamas were among the least important of Britain's thirty-five colonial territories. Though conveniently situated to the American mainland – they were no more than half an hour's flight from Miami – this infertile outpost of empire hardly merited the presence of the man who had once been King. All the same, the Duke was determined to do his job well, which he did on the whole, in spite of such disadvantages as an economy reliant on tourism (which dried up the moment the United States joined the war), a strict colour bar, and a Mafia-like oligarchy that regarded the islands as its own private playground. Still the Duke did what he could; boosting agricultural production, founding a badly needed infant welfare clinic, presiding over the establishment of a war base on the island of New Providence, and quelling civil disorder when black labourers rioted over low earnings.

The Duchess, too, despite upsetting local worthies by likening the Bahamas to Elba and St Helena, won great admiration, not least for her work as President of the Red Cross, a far from honorary position in view of the fact that survivors from ships torpedoed by U-boats were brought to Nassau. Later on the Duchess ran a canteen for American servicemen and won their devotion.

The Duke and Duchess at Government House, Nassau

In fact, the response to the Duke and Duchess whilst in the Bahamas, albeit on a much smaller and less significant scale, was similar to that which the King and Queen met in embattled Britain. Speaking of the Duchess, for instance, one unnamed Lieutenant, who was detailed to look after the Governor and his Lady when they first arrived, said: 'She has, to an infinite degree, that great gift of making you feel that you are the very person she has been waiting all her life to meet. With old & young & clever & stupid alike she exercises this charm. . . . I never saw anyone who could resist the spell – they were all delighted & intrigued.' It is interesting to remember that, almost word for word, the very same has been said repeatedly through the years of Queen Elizabeth the Queen Mother.

Yet if there were those who were impressed by the Duke and Duchess of Windsor during their 'reign' in the Bahamas, there were just as many who were not. Perhaps the greatest criticism of the Duke himself centred upon the unsolved murder of Sir Harry Oakes, a self-made millionaire whom the Windsors befriended. Lady Mosley tells us that the Duke 'was very partial to millionaires who had made their money themselves. Any fool can inherit money, it was self-made men who had glamour for him. He felt about them as an ordinary snob might feel about people of ancient lineage going back into the mists of time.'

Harry Oakes, therefore, was exactly the kind of rough diamond the Duke of Windsor admired, though as with almost any self-made man, he clearly had his enemies and, during the early hours of 8 July 1943, Oakes was brutally murdered by one of them. Four deep holes in his head suggested that he had been attacked with a four-pronged instrument of some kind, while his assailant had then tried to burn the body where it lay. While the real murderer ran free, however, Sir Harry's son-in-law, Alfred de Marigny, was apprehended, charged, and brought to trial. Four months later, he was found not guilty.

Through all this, the Duke of Windsor was criticized for calling in the FBI, rather than the CID – even though the former was only half an hour away by plane; for having originally asked the two detectives who had been assigned to look after him on his trips to Miami to start enquiries; for having censored the press, ineffectually as it turned out, and for not ensuring that investigations continued during the four months when de Marigny was being held on the most circumstantial evidence.

✳

On 16 March 1945, some months before the end of the war, the Duke of Windsor tendered his resignation as Governor of the Bahamas. He and the Duchess then spent the summer in the United States, where they had many friends and, indeed, where they were received with honour and much the same kind of affection enjoyed by the royal family in Britain. They were often guests at the White House, and at the start of one visit to Washington, soon after their arrival in the Bahamas, the Windsors were greeted by a cheering crowd some ten thousand strong.

Then it was back to France, to their house on the Boulevard Suchet, the contents of which the Duke and Duchess found perfectly intact, and the Riviera villa of la Croë, where Italian troops, who had occupied only the

garage, had removed nothing save curtains and a few paintings, but had left the gardens thickly strewn with German land-mines. That October the Duke visited his mother in London, staying with her at Marlborough House and accompanying her everywhere she went. He also called upon his brother at Buckingham Palace. The visit was repeated the following January, the object being to discuss a job. Since the Duke was keen to serve his country again, friends suggested that he might act as a kind of unofficial ambassador, specializing in Anglo-American relations. Although carrying no official responsibilities, it would arguably have been a perfect role for the Duke, utilizing the talents for public relations that had made him – and it remains as true today – the most popular and effective Prince of Wales of all time. The message, still ringing as clear as a bell more than a decade after the events of 1936, was that the Establishment – the royal family, the

The Duke with Queen Mary at Marlborough House

The Duke and Duchess of Windsor at Ednam Lodge, Berkshire, October 1946

The Windsors with their cairn terriers at home in Paris, 1949

Government, the Church – wanted the Windsors kept permanently out of the way.

The only changes in the lives of the Duke and Duchess at this time were of a domestic nature. With the expiry of the lease on 24 Boulevard Suchet, they took up residence at the Ritz Hotel in Paris, and from there the search began for a new town house. In 1949, the year in which the Windsors decided to give up la Croë, the Duchess found 85 Rue de la Faisanderie, and there she and the Duke lived for the next four years. Then in 1953, at a nominal rent, the French Government offered them a splendid three-storey mansion, set in its own grounds on the Bois de Boulogne. No. 4 Route du Champ D'Entrainement, once occupied by General de Gaulle, was to become home to the Windsors for the rest of their lives. Here the Duchess, with impeccable taste, created a veritable palace, combining the exquisite classical elegance of the French style with all the comfort of the English.

A spontaneous crowd gathered to cheer the Duke and Duchess when they visited an antique emporium in Fulham, London

The Duchess's portrait by Gerald Brockhurst

The Duchess created a 'palace' for the Duke at their mansion on the Bois de Boulogne

At much the same time, in order to satisfy the Duke's love of the countryside, they discovered and bought an old mill – le Moulin de la Tuilerie – near the village of Gif-sur-Yvette, on the northern slope of the valley of the Chevreuse. By car this was no more than three-quarters of an hour from Paris. It was there that the Duke fulfilled his passion for gardening, and, as he had done at Fort Belvedere during the early 1930s, laid out a magnificent English garden, of which he was justifiably proud.

One of the Windsors' visitors to the Mill during the late 1950s was James Pope-Hennessy, who was then working on his official biography of Queen Mary. His recollections of the visit are as entertaining as they are illuminating. On the evening that the Duke gave his mother's biographer 'a preliminary look' at some of his private papers, he touched upon the subject of his abdication:

'There's a lot of valuable stuff here, you know' [the Duke said]. 'Unlike the Duchess, I am very well documented. But I keep them all under years, not under people. Let's take a look now at 1936.' We began to talk about the Abdication. 'People can say what they like for it or against it, I don't care; but one thing is certain: *I acted in good faith*. And I was treated bloody shabbily.' A random example of this treatment, with which I strongly sympathized, was the fact (attested by receipted bills) that he had produced £4,000 of the £8,000 for the St George's Chapel monument to his father, Queen Mary paying the other half, and he had not even been invited to the dedication of it; nor had it ever been published anywhere that he had contributed.

He spoke of Queen Mary's coldness.

[Pope-Hennessy said:] 'Yes, Sir, I think one of her chief difficulties in understanding your dilemma was the fact that she had never been in love herself.'

'No, I don't think she had. You're right. My mother was a cold woman, a cold woman. And I, you see, I suppose I had never really been in love before. No I hadn't. I thought I had, but I hadn't ever been in love.'

We spent some more time looking through letters in a random fashion, and then went back to the drawing-room. Before we went, he spoke up . . . with extraordinarily moving tired charm: 'Well, I did my best, you know. I tried to bring the Monarchy into touch.'

'But King George and Queen Mary started that, with their industrial tours in 1913 and so on.'

'In a way they did, but not really. And think of my grandfather.' His face lit up mischievously and boyishly: 'Why, look at my grandfather. He'd just sit in the open landau, receive an address, snip a ribbon and declare something open, returning to Knowsley to dine with his girl friends. Didn't even leave that landau. I did my best to change all that.'

✻

Above The Mill — le Moulin de la Tuilerie — the Duke and Duchess's house near Gif-sur-Yvette

Below The Duchess of Windsor created a more informal look for the Mill

Throughout the next twenty years or so, the Duke and Duchess of Windsor appeared to lead idle, aimless lives, pursuing the kind of superficial pleasures that can be bought only by the immensely rich. This at all events was the impression they gave to the world at large. Yet whatever they did in a life to which they had been condemned very largely by the unremitting attitude of Britain's 'old guard', the Duke and Duchess were never forgotten. The cry 'Good Old Teddy' still was raised whenever the Windsors sailed into Southampton; admirers still pressed flowers into the Duchess's hands; and crowds still gathered spontaneously to cheer them.

March 1953: the death of Queen Mary. The Duke of Windsor stands behind the gun-carriage outside Westminster Hall with the Dukes of Edinburgh, Gloucester and Kent, as the Queen's remains are carried in to lie in state

The Duke of Windsor with his adored sister Mary, HRH The Princess Royal

An elegant study of the
ducal couple in the garden
of their house on the Bois de
Boulogne in Paris

Above The Duchess of Windsor throwing dice during a 'gala gambling' cruise aboard the SS *Rotterdam*

Below The Duchess of Windsor relaxing with Jack le Vien's film crew at her home in Paris

The Duke watching dancers at the Paris lido in 1967

The Duke and Duchess of Windsor drive home through the rain. As he grew old, the Duke's features rapidly assumed the look of his Hanoverian forebears, particularly noticeable in this photograph taken during the late 1960s

As Lord Kinross put it: 'The bulk of the British people now felt only goodwill towards a man who had given so much of his youth to his country, and towards the woman who had given him happiness.' Yet despite the warmth of the public's response, that of the royal family remained unchanged. Then, on his seventieth birthday in June 1964, the Duke received a message of congratulations from his eldest niece, the present Queen, whom he had not seen since the funerals of her father, George VI, and his mother, Queen Mary, more than ten years before.

In 1965 the Queen and her uncle met again, this time while the Duke was recovering in the London Clinic from three operations to save the sight in his right eye. As a child in 1936, the then Princess Elizabeth, who had seen her only once, is said to have asked, 'Who *is* Mrs Simpson?' Now almost thirty years later, they met for the first time, and from that point on a slight thaw in the relationship between the royal family and the Duke and Duchess became evident. When in Paris, for instance, younger members of the family, such as Princess Alexandra, who was born on Christmas Day 1936, exactly a fortnight after her uncle's abdication, and the Duke and Duchess of Kent, called upon the Windsors at their house on the Bois.

London, June 1967. The Duke and Duchess exchange a brief, but cordial greeting with the Queen Mother, at the unveiling of a Memorial to Queen Mary

Then, on 7 June 1967, at the Queen's express invitation, the Duke and Duchess of Windsor attended a ceremony on the Mall to mark the centenary of Queen Mary's birth, during which a bronze portrait plaque of her was unveiled on the garden wall of Marlborough House. In itself the unveiling was of little or no significance; the importance of the event lay in the fact that the Duke and Duchess were included in the royal party and that, for the first time in thirty years, the Duchess was accorded public recognition by the sovereign.

The Duchess bidding farewell to the Queen, Prince Philip and Prince Charles, ten days before the Duke's death in May 1972

As she grew older so the Duchess of Windsor seemed to become better looking, albeit with the aid of a cosmetic surgeon. But by 1970 age had visibly started to take its toll of the Duke. From then until his death, he was rarely free from physical discomfort and even severe pain. A year later, as his voice sank to a hoarse whisper, his doctors diagnosed an inoperable cancer of the throat. By the beginning of 1972 it had become clear that the Duke was dying, and during her State Visit to Paris that May, the Queen, accompanied by Prince Philip and Prince Charles, visited the Duke and Duchess at their mansion. Too ill to join his niece in the ground-floor

The Duke demonstrating how to tie the 'Windsor knot', which he had made famous

drawing-room, the Duke was nevertheless determined to maintain some dignity and, though discreetly supervised by his personal physician, Dr Jean Thin, he was briefly allowed to leave his bed, get dressed 'in a jaunty blazer', and receive the Queen in his sitting-room. Ten days later, on 28 May, he died.

The responsibility for bringing the Duke of Windsor's body home to England that summer lay with the Royal Air Force: a mission that with the utmost discretion had been rehearsed over a period of time. At RAF Benson in Oxfordshire, the Queen was formally represented by the Duke and Duchess of Kent, who headed the official delegation assembled to receive the coffin on its arrival. Next day the remains were taken by road to Windsor. In the nave of St George's Chapel, within sight of the tomb of King George V and Queen Mary, the Duke's coffin, draped with his personal standard and surrounded by amber mourning candles in tall black-and-gold holders, was placed on a deep blue catafalque, there to lie in state until the night before the funeral on Monday 5 June.

Not unexpectedly the Duke's death had rekindled many old loyalties and aroused many an old argument. Some felt that the Queen's invitation to the Duchess to stay at Buckingham Palace as her guest until after the funeral was far too little and much too late. Ian Mikardo MP spoke out against the royal family's 'sickening hypocrisy'. They were, he declared, 'falling over themselves to show the corpse the charity which they denied the man'.

Left The Duchess with the Queen after the Duke of Windsor's funeral service

Right The widowed Duchess driving to Windsor for her husband's funeral, 5 June 1972

The Duke and Duchess with two of their pugs at the Mill

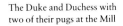

On the evening of 4 June Prince Charles and Lord Mountbatten accompanied the Duchess of Windsor to St George's Chapel. Touching her husband's coffin, she quietly said, 'He was my entire life. I can't begin to think what I am going to do without him; he gave up so much for me.' The following morning, dressed in a simple black coat that Hubert de Givenchy had had made for her in a single night, her face covered by a full black veil, the Duchess left Buckingham Palace shortly after ten o'clock for Windsor Castle. An hour later, seated next to the Queen in the Quire of St George's Chapel, she watched as the Duke's coffin was brought from the Albert Memorial Chapel near by, borne in on the shoulders of officers of The Prince of Wales Company, 1st Battalion Welsh Guards, and followed by the royal princes.

At the close of the service, the Duchess, accompanied by the Queen, the Queen Mother, and members of the royal family, drove slowly through the park to Frogmore. There, in the private burial ground, watched over by a bronze figure of Christ, the Duke of Windsor was interred.

A year later the Duchess returned and, together with Lord Mountbatten and the Duke of Kent, son of her husband's favourite brother Prince George, she visited the Duke's grave, now covered with a simple ledger stone on which, beneath an incised cross, were engraved the words:

HRH The Prince Edward Albert Christian
George Andrew Patrick David, Duke of Windsor
Born 23rd June 1894, Died 28th May 1972
King Edward VIII from January to December 1936

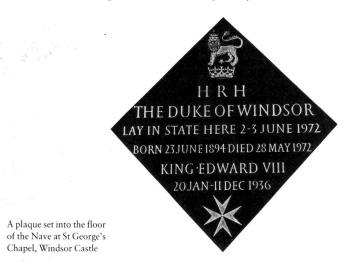

A plaque set into the floor of the Nave at St George's Chapel, Windsor Castle

11 July 1973. The Duchess of Windsor with Lord Mountbatten and the Duke of Kent at her husband's grave at Frogmore

It is said that life for the Duchess of Windsor ended on the day her husband died. Already frail, she started to become yet more so during the early years of her widowhood. Her mind, too, which even then had begun to wander, rapidly deteriorated, so much so that she seemed at times to border on insanity. For a year or two, while she attempted to adjust to life on her own, the Duchess kept up some semblance of normality, visiting America in the spring as she and the Duke always had, arranging social events, entertaining her surviving friends, and so on. But according to her butler 'Monsieur Georges' she was 'never the same again . . . she never overcame the sadness'. At night the Duchess would sit in her husband's room, where everything was kept just as it had been when he was alive. Before retiring she would look around her, then whisper, 'Good-night David.'

Late in 1975, by which time she was already handicapped by the inexorable progress of arteriosclerosis, the Duchess suffered a massive intestinal haemorrhage. She survived but, almost paralysed and bereft of her mental and physical faculties, she became a bedridden recluse, locked in a pitiful world of shadows. Diana Mosley, who used sometimes to sit with the Duchess, wrote that the last time she saw her 'her face looked like the Greek mask of Tragedy, her mouth a square, her dark and penetrating blue eyes staring out of the window'. Towards the end, even the Duchess's closest friends were discouraged from visiting, because her inability to communicate with them caused her considerable anxiety and distress.

At the Queen's request the British Ambassador in Paris kept Her Majesty informed of the Duchess's condition. From time to time there were false alarms and rumours that she was being kept alive artificially. However, as one of her friends who was always kept informed of her progress told the author in December 1985, 'Such stories are completely untrue. The simple fact of the matter is that her heart is so strong, it simply refuses to die.'

Death finally came to Wallis, Duchess of Windsor, at 10 a.m. on Thursday 24 April 1986, the cause being ascribed to pulmonary pneumonia. Three days later, contained in a heavy coffin of dark English oak, its lid covered with a mass of madonna lilies, the body of the Duchess, whose ninetieth birthday would have fallen on 19 June, was flown from Paris to RAF Benson, where the Duke of Gloucester waited to receive it. From Oxfordshire the coffin was driven to Windsor Castle where on the shoulders of eight Welsh Guardsmen, it was borne up the West Steps of St George's Chapel and slowly carried through to the Albert Memorial Chapel, where it rested until the day of the funeral.

At 2.15 on the afternoon of 29 April, a small procession led by the Dean of Windsor, Dr Michael Mann, and the Military Knights of Windsor, who mounted a vigil, brought the coffin to a catafalque in front of the high altar in St George's Chapel. Little more than an hour later, members of the royal family, led by the Queen, Prince Philip and Queen Elizabeth The Queen Mother (who had always been the Duchess's most bitter opponent), joined a small congregation that included Viscount Whitelaw, representing the Prime Minister, and such friends of the Duchess of Windsor as Grace, Countess of Dudley, Lady Mosley, and Lady Alexandra Metcalfe, at the start of the dignified, but sadly impersonal, funeral service.

Borne on the shoulders of eight Welsh Guardsmen, the Duchess's coffin leaves St George's Chapel, Windsor, after the funeral service on 29 April 1986

The choir sang the Sentences, 'I am the resurrection and the life.' The Dean read the Lesson from 2 Corinthians, containing the sharply poignant words, 'We know that so long as we are at home in the body we are exiles from the Lord.' One hymn, 'Lead us Heavenly Father, lead us', was sung, the Archbishop of Canterbury pronounced a blessing, and then, as the Chapel echoed to the haunting strains of *Nimrod*, the exquisite central adagio from Elgar's 'Enigma Variations', the coffin was borne out and placed in the waiting hearse for the short journey to Frogmore. There the Duchess of Windsor was buried in a simple grave next to that of her husband.

When the funeral party had departed, the floral tributes were briefly displayed in the Horseshoe Cloisters in front of the West Steps of St George's Chapel. On one, an informal handwritten message from the Duke and Duchess of Kent was simply signed 'Eddie and Katharine'; on another a formal, typed card read: 'From Her Royal Highness Princess Alice, Duchess of Gloucester, and Their Royal Highnesses the Duke and Duchess of Gloucester.' There were wreaths from Diana Mosley and Diana Vreeland, and a flamboyant tribute from Estée Lauder, head of the perfume house that bears her name. There were also many anonymous floral arrangements, some from complete strangers, such as that which bore the inscription 'The Heart Has Its Reasons', a reminder of the title of the Duchess's autobiography; one 'To a Gracious Lady, from a Bristol family'; and one which recalled the Duke and Duchess's years in the Bahamas. Signed 'RAF Unit III 1942 to 1945 – Now Nassau Association', the message contained a verse which read:

> Gentle treasures of memories fall,
> Heartfelt remembrances from us all,
> Rest in peace our dear Duchess,
> From your ex-Royal Air Force Boys
> in the Bahamas.

∗

At a distance of fifty years, to ask whether the Duchess of Windsor was in truth the avaricious good-time girl of popular legend, or a victim of unhappy circumstance, is largely academic. What is and always will remain of the utmost importance, is the way in which she rose to meet the unenviable demands of her role as the wife and consort of an appallingly weak man; a man too enfeebled by ruthless royal strictures to cope with life alone. If only in retrospect there can be no doubt that there would always have been a burning need in Edward VIII's life for a Wallis Simpson of some description, just as in the life of his successor, George VI, there existed the very same need for an Elizabeth Bowes Lyon. Both princes yearned for the love and support of dominant women, and both women satisfied those needs entirely. Yet while Elizabeth, Duchess of York, was accorded all the honour long considered to be royalty's due and, as Queen, earned the almost unreserved affection of the nation, Wallis, Duchess of Windsor, was subjected to the grossest calumny and ever denied the royal status that was arguably hers by right.

As John Grigg (the former Lord Altrincham) wrote in *The Times* the day after the Duchess's death, the idea that the Abdication 'cheapened or undermined the institution [of monarchy] is fantasy'. Today, in spite of the rights and wrongs of the issue, it cannot be denied that the Abdication ultimately served to strengthen the monarchy to an extraordinarily vigorous degree. That was the service Edward VIII and Wallis Simpson rendered the Crown. That should be their epitaph.

BIBLIOGRAPHY

Airlie, Mabell, Countess of. *Thatched with Gold*, Hutchinson, 1962.

Bloch, Michael (ed.). *Wallis & Edward Letters*, Weidenfeld & Nicolson, 1986.

Bryan III, J. and Murphy, Charles J. V. *The Windsor Story*, Granada, 1979.

Cooper, Diana. *The Light of Common Day*, Michael Russell, 1979.

Donaldson, Frances. *Edward VIII*, Weidenfeld & Nicolson, 1974.

Hardinge, Helen. *Loyal to Three Kings*, William Kimber, 1967.

Holroyd, Michael. *Lytton Strachey: The Years of Achievement 1910–1932*, Heinemann, 1968.

Huxley, Elspeth. *Out in the Midday Sun*, Chatto & Windus, 1985.

James, Robert Rhodes (ed.). *Chips: The Diaries of Sir Henry Channon*, Penguin, 1984.

Lord Kinross. *The Windsor Years*, Penguin, 1980.

Longford, Elizabeth. *The Royal House of Windsor*, Weidenfeld & Nicolson, 1974.

Mosley, Diana. *The Duchess of Windsor*, Sidgwick & Jackson, 1980.

Olsen, Stanley (ed.). *Harold Nicolson: Diaries and Letters 1930–1964*, Penguin, 1980.

Pope-Hennessy, James. *Queen Mary*, Allen & Unwin, 1959.

Quennell, Peter (ed.). *A Lonely Business*, Weidenfeld & Nicolson, 1980.

Rose, Kenneth. *King George V*, Papermac, 1983.

  Kings, Queens and Courtiers, Weidenfeld & Nicolson, 1985.

Vickers, Hugo. *Cecil Beaton*, Weidenfeld & Nicolson, 1985.

Warwick, Christopher. *King George VI and Queen Elizabeth*, Sidgwick & Jackson, 1985.

Wheeler-Bennett, John W. *King George VI: His Life and Reign*, Macmillan, 1958.

Windsor, The Duchess of. *The Heart Has Its Reasons*, Michael Joseph, 1956

Windsor, HRH The Duke of. *A King's Story*, Cassell, 1951

Zeigler, Philip. *Mountbatten*, Collins, 1985.

The Times, Daily Telegraph, Daily Mail, Daily Express, Illustrated London News.

INDEX

PICTURE ACKNOWLEDGEMENTS

The author and publisher have made every effort to trace the copyright in the photographs that
appear in this book. The publishers would like to thank the following who have been particularly
helpful in supplying black and white pictures and allowing their reproduction in this book:
Mr Hugo Vickers, 28, 92, 83, 104, 107, 113, 131, 132 (left and right), 140, 144, 159
The Honourable Mrs Angela Lascelles: 70 (top and bottom)
Patrick Lichfield: 164
The Author: 11, 44 (top right), 124

The publishers would also like to thank:
Associated Press: 162
Camera Press: 33, 35, 38, 84 (top left), 150, 158, 160 (bottom), 163, 167
Illustrated London News: 24, 45 (right), 49, 50, 63, 66, 94, 128
Press Association: 149, 169
Popperfoto: 10, 17, 18, 20, 22, 29, 32 (left and right), 42, 47, 54, 55, 57, 59 (top and bottom), 61,
68, 71, 74, 78, 80 (top and bottom), 89, 91, 96 (top and bottom), 100 (left and right), 101, 137,
142, 146, 148, 151, 154 (top and bottom), 157, 159 (top), 161, 165 (left and right)
Syndication International: 153
Topham Picture Library: 15, 16, 40, 45 (left), 93, 115, 116, 119 (top and bottom), 134, 136, 152,
156, 160

Colour Section (between pages 64 and 65, in order of appearance)
Reproduced by gracious permission of Her Majesty the Queen: His Royal Highness, Prince
Edward in cadet uniform aged fourteen.
Prince Edward in his Garter robes in 1912, one year after he was created Prince of Wales.
Mr Hugo Vickers: Wallis Simpson at forty: a portrait; Cecil Beaton's watercolour sketch of Wallis
Simpson, 1936; Edward VIII, 'the first English king to fly'.
The coat-of-arms of HRH The Duke of Windsor.
Camera Press: The Duke and Duchess of Windsor, photographed by Karsh of Ottawa;
The Duchess of Windsor at the age of seventy-five, photographed by Karsh of Ottawa;
The Duke of Windsor's coffin arriving at RAF Benson in Oxfordshire.
Popperfoto: The Duke and Duchess in the garden of the Mill, le Moulin de la Tuilerie.
Press Association: The lying-in-state of the Duke of Windsor, June 1972.